Andrea Adams was ⟨. ..⟩ nce broadcaster ⟨. ..⟩ who spent three y⟨ear⟩ ⟨...⟩ ⟨cov⟩ering the effects ⟨...⟩ ⟨bully⟩ing at work. Her first presentation of this phenome⟨non w⟩as in two BBC Radio 4 documentaries, 'An Abuse ⟨of Po⟩wer' and 'Whose Fault Is It Anyway?' The programmes elicited a tremendous public response of which this book is a direct result. Andrea died in 1995 having substantially raised the profile of workplace bullying in Britain.

Neil Crawford, author of several chapters in this book, trained as a psychoanalytic psychotherapist at the Tavistock Clinic, London, where he is a senior consultant in the Tavistock Consultation Service. He is a leading expert in this field, consulting to organisations, lecturing and running management seminars on workplace bullying and human relations in organisations.

Andrea Adams

BULLYING

AT WORK

How to confront and overcome it

**With contributions from
Neil Crawford**

A *Virago* Book

First published by Virago Press 1992

Reprinted 1994, 1995, 1996, 1998, 2000

A CIP catalogue record for this book is
available from the British Library

ISBN 1 85381 542 X

Printed and bound in Great Britain by
Clays Ltd, St Ives plc

Virago
A Division of
Little, Brown and Company (UK)
Brettenham House
Lancaster Place
London WC2E 7EN

For my parents, Philip and Dulcie,
who gave me life, and unstinting love.

Humanity will ever seek but never attain perfection.
Let us at least survive and go on trying.
Dora Russell, 'The Religion of the Machine Age'

Contents

Author's Note   ix

Acknowledgements   x

Is This Book for You?   1

Foreword   3

Part One: The Problem   7

  1 Forewarned is Forearmed   9

  2 Seeing is Believing   15

  3 Fact not Fiction   22

  4 Bossy or Bully?   30

  5 The Bullied   38

      Helping yourself   58

Part Two: The Causes   67

  6 The Psychology of the Bully   69
      by Neil Crawford

  7 The Bullies   87

  8 The Psychology of the Bullied   96
      by Neil Crawford

      Helping yourself   107

Part Three: Seeking Solutions   111

  9 Fighting Back   113

 10 Getting It Right   134

 11 Organisational Responsibility   152
      by Neil Crawford

 12 Managing People Properly   167

      Helping yourself   181

Endpiece   185

Further Reading   188
Routes to Recovery   190
Organisations and Addresses   193
General Reading   194

Author's Note

All the women and men in this book are real individuals whom I interviewed in depth, or corresponded with. All quotes are used with their consent. In order to protect their livelihoods, however, their names, and the names of their family members, have been changed. Other identifying details, as well as geographical locations and specific job descriptions, have been slightly altered or omitted.

Acknowledgements

I would particularly like to thank all those men and women whose determination to speak out enabled me to tap an endless source of real experience for the benefit of this book; Cathy Drysdale, Tim Suter and Michael Green at the BBC, who were the first to support my view that adult bullying was a major issue which should be exposed; more recently, my editor, Melanie Silgardo, who recognised an opportunity to improve the quality of our working lives by inviting me to expand the subject still further. I am also grateful to Francis Spencer, teacher and poet, who patiently helped me focus my thoughts, and to Tim Page, M.I.P.M., for his valuable comment and professional wisdom. I would also like to thank John Steele, Richard Worsley and their employers, British Telecom, for their encouragement and support throughout my research into this subject; Ann Williams, psychotherapist, for giving me added insight into the realms of human suffering; also Ben and Belinda Brocklehurst, who provided inspirational surroundings on the Greek island of Lefkas, enabling me to get the writing under way; Gemini and Jacob Adams for their love, support and insistence that I could write a book whenever I panicked and said I couldn't! Finally, I would like to say a belated thank you to Ted Coleman, a former editor of the *Skegness Standard*, whose firm, fair and encouraging approach made him an excellent first boss.

Is This Book for You?

- You feel under stress at work because whatever you do is belittled by your boss
- Your confidence has been undermined and your health affected
- Your partner seems depressed and wants to talk only about the way the boss behaves at work
- As a child you were frequently criticised but rarely praised
- At work you think you are always right and like to keep everyone else under your control
- Your organisation has a rapid staff turnover, rising sickness and absenteeism rates
- Profits and productivity have inexplicably declined

Foreword

In June 1989 Andrea Adams came to me with an alarming story. It sounded incredible, and would have been especially hard to believe if it hadn't affected so many people. Over a period of four years, no less than fifty men and women employed at a major high street bank had had their working days made utterly miserable by one of their managers. He had persistently intimidated and humiliated selected individuals, with the result that their personal and professional confidence was severely undermined. Despite attempts by his staff to stand up to him, and despite the numerous complaints that were made to personnel, nothing was done. Yet if his behaviour was having such a devastating effect, why was it allowed to continue, unchecked and disbelieved, for so long?

For a radio producer, original ideas are vital, but they must be about something to which listeners can relate, and although I was intrigued by this story, I remained sceptical. Could it really be that the trivial behaviour we usually associate with the school bully was terrorising men and women at their place of work?

In the months that followed, bullying hit the headlines. A child was murdered in a Manchester school playground. Kidscape, a charity concerned with children's welfare, issued guidelines for dealing with bullies at school. Education authorities began to encourage new policies to deal with the problem. The media covered efforts by the Ministry of Defence to stamp it out in the armed forces. No one, however, was talking about bullying anywhere else.

Once Andrea's preliminary research had indicated that

the problem in the workplace could be widespread, we were given the go-ahead to make a two-part radio investigation. But even at this stage, I can clearly recall my apprehension when I sat down to hear the first of her recorded interviews. For any producer that first 'listen' is always exciting, but this time my anticipation was mixed with anxiety. Would I be genuinely convinced by the story I heard, or would I have to conclude that this was a person who seemed to encounter trouble wherever they worked?

Ten minutes into the first tape I was doodling on the pad in front of me beginning to feel irritated. Anne, a woman bank employee, recounted how her manager had ridiculed her in front of the others for her vegetarian eating habits. Her response at once suggested that Anne must be over-sensitive. Did she really have to resort to eating her lunch in the ladies' loo to escape his taunts? Surely she could have withstood something so petty? Had I made a mistake in proposing this programme? As it transpired, she was not alone, and as she catalogued the verbal destruction of many other members of staff, a picture of the manager in question slowly emerged: an autocrat capable of extreme unpleasantness who was mercilessly aggressive and frequently out of control.

Although this was two years after his removal from the bank, Anne's voice still trembled. 'You feel so demeaned, inadequate somehow . . . because it teaches you things about yourself that you are not very proud of . . . that you should have been stronger . . . that you shouldn't accept what is thrown at you when you know instinctively that it is wrong.' Within thirty minutes of pressing the playback button, I, too, was in tears, and although I didn't realise it at the time, my experience of listening to that first recording was to take me through all the stages of disbelief – and the need for proof – that besets all those who suffer from being bullied at work.

Despite this early initiation, Andrea and I were completely unprepared for the response which followed the two radio programmes. Most of these women and men had never before felt able to tell their stories, even though some of the incidents they recalled had taken place twenty years earlier. Letters were filled with painful revelations. Telephone calls were distressing in their detail. If this unprecedented response was an indication, the scale of the problem was frightening. Teachers, nurses, personnel staff, civil servants, clergymen, union employees, secretaries, managing directors, shop assistants – few areas of employment were exempt. Contrary to my original anxieties, many of these people had done everything in their power to stand up for themselves, even though the penalty for telling tales was to risk putting their jobs on the line. In which case, you may wonder why the problem was not already exposed.

It became clear that bullying has nasty connotations, for some of us disturbing memories of things that have happened to us in other contexts. It was embarrassing to talk about, even to close colleagues, so people became isolated from each other once they were repeatedly under attack. The predicament of all those involved raised important questions, which this book endeavours to answer. Why do some people misuse their personal power over others? What can those on the receiving end do to defend themselves? Are any of us likely targets? Are we all potential bullies? Can childhood experiences be blamed for the way we behave when we go to work? What is the employer's responsibility when caring for the psychological well-being of all employees?

It is my belief that in every organisation, every company, someone is likely to be experiencing the difficulties imposed by bullying behaviour that has not been identified. This book is an attempt to find a way forward; through personal accounts which detail every aspect of the dilemmas faced by all those involved; through the eyes of psychotherapist, Neil Crawford, who helped us in our programmes to understand the reasons why. Whether you are being bullied, or suspect you are a bully yourself;

5

whether you have been approached to help someone, or whether you wish to prevent bullying from occurring within your area of concern – this book has been written for you. I hope it will also serve as a tribute to those courageous women and men who, three years ago, trusted us with their painful stories. I hope they will feel we have used their experiences to good effect.

Cathy Drysdale, BBC Radio 4
Producer, *An Abuse of Power* and
Whose Fault is it Anyway?
1992

PART ONE

The Problem

He is a human being and terrible
things are happening to him. So
attention must be paid.
Arthur Miller, *Death of a Salesman*

1
Forewarned is Forearmed

*Facts do not cease to exist
because they are ignored.*
Aldous Huxley, *Proper Studies 'Note on Dogma'*

Imagine. It's Monday morning and you leave for work with a sickening feeling in the pit of your stomach. Anxiety has disturbed another night's sleep. All you can think about is another week of being persistently undermined at work.

It is shocking to discover that respected working colleagues can subject you to the petty criticisms and name-calling that you thought you had seen the last of when you left school. For that reason, adults on the receiving end are often ashamed to admit that they can't cope. Like the child bullied at school, they become convinced that what is happening to them is their fault.

Bullying at work is like a malignant cancer. It creeps up on you long before you – or anyone else – are able to appreciate what it is that is making you feel the ill effects. Yet despite the fact that the majority of the adult population spends more waking hours at work than anywhere else, the disturbing manifestations of adult bullying, in this particular context, are widely dismissed.

Kate held an important post in a government advisory service, where her boss's relentless bullying eventually caused her to become so ill that she was advised to take prolonged sick leave:

9

'It started at my induction interview, when in front of a colleague he said, "Well, you might look all right, but we don't know if you've got a brain in your head, do we?" Later I heard him make similar comments to some of the men. He was constantly making derogatory statements, to the point where I felt totally bewildered and wondered why on earth he was so against me. Everything I did was called into question. He listened in to telephone calls, invented complaints from outside contacts which proved to be totally unfounded, and then told me I was a lovely person who was reading too much into his actions.

'Despite the fact that I was doing what was required, and senior colleagues confirmed that I was doing it right, he created the myth that I was a hopeless and inadequate person. One morning I arrived at work and found my office empty. He'd moved my desk into a colleague's office as punishment for receiving one personal telephone call. It was disorientating and I just never knew what I was going into the next day. When I went into hospital for an operation, he told everyone in the office that I wasn't genuinely ill and I realised that if he couldn't get rid of me for something I hadn't done, he was going to invent things. I began to feel very distressed and threatened, but because he'd been there for so long, and was a personal friend of the director, I knew that if I complained, he would be the one to be believed.'

Although some people will insist otherwise, bullying at work is separate from the recognised problems of sexual harassment or racism. A male colleague who had previously worked for Kate's boss, for example, resigned because his health was so adversely affected. He was repeatedly insulted, and his annual report was judged on damning personal events which simply had not happened. When he finally left, he was on the verge of a nervous breakdown. Other men in that office were also singled out

10

for demeaning words and deeds, and as the stories in this book unfold, you will discover that female bullies are no less vitriolic, wherever they work. (*See Chapter 9 for the outcome of Kate's experiences.*)

Before Hilda's appointment as manager of a medium-sized office in the public sector, staff left only for personal reasons or better-paid jobs. Less than three months after her arrival, the previously high morale was virtually destroyed. One year after her rampant bullying began, resignations and transfers had depleted the office of an experienced workforce. Two of her colleagues provide a portrait of a typical bullying style:

'When Hilda arrived she said she was prepared to listen to people's views and opinions. In fact she employed a practice of shouting down or talking over those who disagreed with her and subsequently labelled them blinkered. Her manner was intimidating from the outset and she seemed determined that she would brook no opposition from anyone. "You *will* do this" and "I *won't* have that" were two of her favourite phrases. Hilda gradually became less aloof with staff when she realised that not communicating with them meant having less control. Then she took to asking people loaded questions about each other. These were later referred to as undisclosed sources of information which, in turn, created tension and distrust.

'She passed down most of her instructions through supervisors and constantly changed working guidelines and procedures without any consultation so that people became confused, overworked and frequently distressed by these bewildering alterations. Hilda also had a knack of making staff feel that if they didn't do what she wanted, in the way that she wanted, and within the time *she* said it would take, they were inefficient. This made people fearful of making errors, or being caught in the backlash of those committed by colleagues, soon causing friction in an office where previously everyone had worked well. Her tyrannical approach often reduced grown men and women to a state of running around like headless chickens, desperately trying to solve a problem before there were further recriminations. People were snapping at each other all the time because of the pressure.

'Hilda continues to insist on taking control of even the most trivial aspects of office procedure, but at the expense of important management checks. It's as if she feels that to let go of the smallest thing would mean that control of everything would begin to slip from her hands. She appears to perceive anyone else's comments or opinions as a threat which must be removed. Her selective memory means that she chooses to remember only people's bad points and flagrantly abuses the annual reporting system to make personal attacks. Hilda is also capable of being charming and good-humoured, and this is the side that outsiders always see.'

Numerous complaints about Hilda's behaviour were made to personnel and welfare officers, and assurances were given that some positive action would be taken to help her to become more reasonable. Nine months later, nothing had been done to improve the situation and further resignations followed.

In view of the fact that bullying in apparently respectable places of work is allowed to continue unchecked, it is perhaps no surprise that the problem is something with which, at the time of writing this book, no organisation wished to be publicly identified. But whether the label is denied or not, bullying at work is emerging as an alarmingly widespread phenomenon. In order to solve a problem, however, you have to be able to recognise it, and in order to recognise it, you must be able to give it a name.

Harassment, intimidation, aggression, bad attitude,

coercive management, personality clash, poor management style, 'brutalism' and even 'working in a funny way' are labels more commonly used. In America, employee abuse, as it is called, is referred to as 'workplace trauma', but it has been identified as a more crippling and devastating problem for employees and employers than all the other work-related stresses put together.

On both sides of the Atlantic, failure to recognise the problem as it really is has already proved a hugely expensive error, both in financial terms and in the way that individuals' belief in themselves as useful members of the workforce is eroded. Statistical evaluation will clearly have to wait until organisations confront the issue and its effects. At present, bullying is not singled out as one of the greatest sources of stress which causes people to stay away from work through fear, or to take prolonged sick leave. Costly training is money down the drain when employees resign from their jobs simply to escape. There is no doubt that for this reason alone they leave in droves, taking with them a sense of injustice that the person who has made their working lives a misery is the one who nearly always remains. Yet the boss who bullies is often someone whose innermost feelings of inadequacy and insecurity can be a serious threat to the effective running of any organisation, particularly when that person is put under stress or overstretched.

The costs to the individual are explored in personal accounts throughout this book. As yet it is impossible to identify the precise costs to industry or other organisations because, as in cases of unreported rape, there can be no statistics to quantify the true scale. However, given the physical and emotional effects of those who suffer this experience, the likelihood is that a sizeable percentage of the following examples will be directly attributable to unidentified bullying at work.

- Over 360 million working days are lost each year through ill health, according to the Department of Health.

- In the UK, the Confederation of British Industry puts the annual cost of stress-related absenteeism and staff turnover at £1.3 billion.
- For an individual business, the effects of stress-related problems could amount to 5 or 10 per cent of profits, according to Professor Cary Cooper, Professor of Organisational Psychology at the University of Manchester Institute of Science and Technology.
- In the United States, the Bureau of National Affairs states that businesses are losing an annual five to six billion dollars in decreased productivity alone caused by real or perceived abuse of employees (*Personnel Journal*, July 1991).

To protect all employees, and their own financial interests for the future, organisations must surely be persuaded to examine more closely the climate in which they expect people to work. In Britain, stress audits and employee assistance counselling programmes are still in their infancy, yet both provide a confidential outlet for men and women to tell it how it really is.

A study of Post Office workers in the North of England revealed a 66 per cent reduction in absenteeism after such counselling sessions. The exercise showed that for every 175 people counselled, there was a saving to the organisation of £1,000. In the United States, where employee assistance programmes are comparatively commonplace, a random sample of 600 full-time workers showed that 72 per cent said they suffered from three or more stress-related symptoms – highlighting the need, perhaps, to dig deeper and establish when it is bullying that is the major source.

2
Seeing is Believing

When regard for truth has been broken down or even slightly weakened, all things will remain doubtful.
St Augustine 'On Lying'

To make a convincing complaint about what is happening at work, you first have to know exactly what is going wrong. But before you even take that route, there can be other hurdles to overcome. In an essentially macho organisation, for example, weakness is despised, and until the problem becomes more generally identified the likelihood is that bullying will be suffered in silence.

Defy the bully and risk losing promotion, resign and jeopardise financial security, report the person's behaviour to a higher authority and end up being branded as lacking in resolve. Without adequate recourse for those caught up in this catch-22 situation, there is often too much at stake to tell tales.

Jamie, an ex-army officer:
'It isn't easy to shrug off the pressures imposed by the bullying superior; the working all hours to meet questionable deadlines, the nitpicking, the demand for ultra-perfection in trivial matters; insidious time-wasting in normal working hours so that the real work can be done only after the bully has gone home; the miserable atmosphere of the workplace when all the staff are on the receiving end; disruption to family life. If it's happening at the height of a person's ambitions, when their family and financial commitments make

15

them most vulnerable, small wonder that the individual feels trapped and the bully survives unchallenged.'

C. Brady Wilson,* a clinical psychologist in Arizona, has made a study of the profound effects of abuse on employees and states: 'it clearly falls under the domain of post-traumatic stress disorder, similar to the shell shock suffered by soldiers experiencing battle conditions'. There is no doubt that once bullying gets a grip, the employers should focus their attention on possible clues, such as a high staff turnover, absenteeism, prolonged sick leave, and a decline in productivity.

The earliest signal to the individual is when a relationship at work somehow doesn't *feel* right. Problems often arise when a person is newly appointed, or internally promoted to a position, so if professional contributions which have previously been respected and appreciated suddenly become the target for continual criticism, someone should wonder why.

The individual's responsibility is to ask: How does this person respond to me in a different way from my previous boss? Do I suddenly feel put down? Being aware of what might be happening to you early on puts you in a stronger position to counter belittling remarks, or fend off attacks on your professional competence. If you feel that the situation is not something you can handle yourself, observing the differences in behaviour will at least equip you to explain your dilemma to those above your boss.

There is no doubt that being bullied at work leaves both men and women feeling very hurt, vulnerable, angry and impotent – not least because the boss is usually the one to be believed. But if it is a person's perception that they are being bullied, then the bottom line is that *they* must be believed. If they are not, all their time and energy

* Quoted in 'US Businesses Suffer from Workplace Trauma', *Personnel Journal*, July 1991

will be used up in simply trying to survive each working day, in the knowledge that whatever they do is likely to come under attack, or be undermined.

Bullying at work, like bullying at school, often takes place where there are no witnesses. Without concrete evidence, however, proof is almost impossible. If others are not present, or if colleagues are too concerned about their own jobs to back up any complaint about a bullying boss, it is crucial to keep a detailed diary and log everything that has been said or done to you during the time you feel you have been bullied. Without third-party proof, this is one way of putting together a case.

Recognition is a major problem because bullying is rarely confined to derisory remarks or open aggression. It can be subtle, devious and immensely difficult to confront for those whose confidence and self-esteem have been exposed to a misuse of personal power and position. One of the reasons why the problem occurs at all is envy, usually of a quality that the bully does not possess. The background to this will be explained in a later chapter, but it is important to bear in mind that a bully will probably try to get rid of someone whom he or she perceives as any sort of threat to their own position within an organisation. The ways of achieving this can be so subtle as to go entirely undetected, so here are some clues:

- A manager may not promote a very able subordinate, for example, because of a fear that they might prove more competent and ultimately take over their job. By overlooking a person in this way, the bully can keep them in their place so that they no longer pose a professional threat.
- A manager who takes the credit for somebody else's ideas is likely to make a subordinate feel that their initiative is being undervalued. The underlying hope is that constantly stifling any chance for creativity, so that life is made intolerable, will cause the person concerned to leave their job through sheer frustration.

17

Getting rid of the competition is a classic survival technique.

- A manager may alter objectives, knowing that the new ones cannot be achieved. Once there is evidence that the person has failed to meet the requirements of his or her job, the perfect excuse to bring about dismissal becomes available.

So – if you *feel* that things are going wrong in a working relationship, what do you do? To tackle unseen aggression in particular, you need to be aware of what it actually is. The following set of experiences will help you to identify ways in which a bullying boss may set out to undermine . . .

Janet, a deputy headteacher:

'Almost from day one I realised my move to a new school had been a mistake. Within the first hour I saw staff being verbally torn apart by our boss. I also discovered there was very little for me to do. Aware of my high academic qualifications, and my proven success in running another school, she gradually encouraged me to apply for headships. Then she'd tell me she couldn't give me anything substantial to do within the school because I might be leaving, so I was only given menial tasks. When I needed her support for applications I'd made, she said she couldn't give me a good reference because I hadn't put anything into the school. When I was eventually asked by the head to produce an educational document, colleagues told me it was the most exciting thing to come out of the place in years, and it created much excitement and enthusiasm within the academic environment. But my ideas were always attributed to someone else, and as soon as the head saw me succeeding, and enjoying what I was doing, she'd take it away halfway through and give it to someone more junior.'

Steve, an employee of an American company based in Britain:

'Where I work there is extensive bullying as part of a hiring and firing policy. One technique is to make people redundant and then have a change of mind. This happened to me, and I'm still there because if I leave out of annoyance, I lose any redundancy money. When the same thing happened to a colleague who'd been with the company for eighteen years, he was given one hour to leave the premises. Many people I know were given the same treatment, with the same timescale, including one guy who'd notched up twenty-seven years' service. Replacements are always found for these employees, often with slightly different grades or job descriptions. Another common technique is to promote someone to a new post, appoint someone to fill their previous job, and then, after a year or so, declare the new post redundant. Perhaps the company's most disturbing bullying tactic is demotion for no justifiable reason.'

Suzanne, a civil servant:

'He was always moving the goalposts so that we could never anticipate what he wanted to show up on any particular job. If we pointed out these inconsistencies, which were clearly deliberate, he either flatly denied his previous decisions or told us that we must have misunderstood what he had said. He Snopaked or Tippexed out notes that we had made relating to our work, or altered values in our notes, so that there was no record of his changes of mind on policy that we had recorded to cover ourselves. He always made it look as though the extra correctional work was our fault, not his.' (In Chapter 9 Suzanne challenges her bullying boss.)

Anne, a clerk who resigned from a transport network:

'Papers that came through the post for me to record were withheld by this person, so I'd sit at my desk for up to two days with nothing to do and then be shouted at for being lazy. She also took letters out of the Internal Post box which I was sending or receiving, and that sent my work haywire. Completed documents would disappear from my desk, which meant that they had to be redone or I'd get into trouble. She constantly made sneering comments about my working-class background and referred to me as "a member of the lower orders". She talked like that about me to everybody, so I ended up feeling like some sort of non-person. I think she was jealous of younger women because she'd looked after a sick mother for years while her sisters married rich husbands and moved away. What I can't understand is why both the head of department and personnel ignored the constant stream of formal complaints about this woman. They allowed it to go on for years, but people were always being told "Well, she has worked for us for a long, long time".'

Joe, an advertising executive:

'If he thought someone was doing a better job than him, he'd move them out into a cramped office that was well away from everybody else. He wanted to know everything about us, as if we were his property, and we all felt constantly spied on. He'd creep up and listen outside office doors, or suddenly peer through the window. We were convinced the place was bugged because he seemed to know exactly what had been said and done, even when he was away seeing a client. The place was full of paranoia. People were constantly leaving, because in his eyes whatever they did was rarely right."

John, a college lecturer:

'Time and time again she undermined the staff's authority in front of the students, putting us down and trying to prove us wrong. For six years there wasn't

20

one staff meeting or proper discussion, just bits of paper pinned on a door or a noticeboard to tell you what must be done. One time when she was off sick, and I'd been put in overall charge, she suddenly turned up and I found her sitting at my desk with everything moved round. On other occasions I'd arrive to find she'd overturned all my decisions and even telephoned people to make other arrangements.'

Rosemary, a bank clerk:

'If you did overtime, he would strike off your name and say you should have done it in the specified time, so you never got what was due to you. If you challenged him, he would pick on you for the rest of the week, calling you offensive names in front of the others. People became too afraid to act on their own initiative in case it backfired, and a lot of youngsters with promising careers ahead of them ran away because they just couldn't bear it. Staff became so jumpy that they didn't care about each other any more.'

Lyn, a theatre nurse:

'I was always being subjected to witch-hunt assessments, and from day one I was told that I must realise I was a sitting target, with my Yorkshire accent and bleached blonde hair. I'd get a telephone call from the nurses' school at the hospital where I worked, saying the senior tutor wanted to see me, and when I got there I'd be completely alone. On one occasion she said she was sick of me, because every time she went into her office she'd find a note complaining about me. I later found out that this was totally untrue. My mistake was that in class I was over-inquisitive, but the hierarchy in hospitals is the same for everyone. For every person who's kicking you, someone is kicking them from upstairs.'

3
Fact not Fiction

'Human beings are perhaps never more frightening than when they think beyond doubt that they are right.'
Laurens Van der Post, 'The Lost World of Kalahari'

If those at the top of an organisation choose not to be firm with an aggressor, then in a way they are condoning the bullying by allowing it to take place. By ignoring it altogether, they also risk losing the respect of valuable employees. The following story reveals the bizarre and, indeed, hostile response of one organisation when a senior director is accused of being a bully.

First comes denial from the managing director that bullying could even occur without his knowledge. There then begins a series of desperate ploys to safeguard the reputation of a well-known British company which, ironically, specialises in putting other people's houses in order when work processes require improvement. It is, I hope, a salutary example to any organisation of the importance of putting people before profit.

As the drama unfolds, it is Helen who is centre stage. An experienced facilities manager, she is described as highly efficient and very popular among her colleagues; in fact the very linchpin of the main office and all those dependent on her ability to organise.

'My immediate boss was constantly making arrogant and abusive complaints about other employees in my presence, but because I enjoyed my job so much, I simply sat and listened. He used foul language to me, too, but I took a conscious decision to avoid confrontation, to calm him down as best I could for the sake of the other staff, and hope that I'd come out of it relatively unscathed. One day when we were alone together we had a clash of opinion, and because I was sick of absorbing all his complaints, I felt I had to stick up for myself. He was really going for me over a petty office policy of his that was proving difficult to enforce. When I said to him, "Martin, please don't bully me about it," he just exploded. He jumped up in the air and behaved like a lunatic, shouting, "Don't you *dare* use that word with me."

'His raised voice attracted everyone's attention and I became aware of six or seven people watching us through the glass partition. I knew what would be going through their minds because I'd been one of those people, watching others be humiliated and verbally torn to shreds. Now it was my turn, and during that exchange he turned loathsome to me.

'Up till then I was forever excusing his behaviour to the secretaries, convinced that he must have had some sadness in his life, or a lousy childhood, perhaps. Now, he frightened me. "I said I was going to have you out and now you're going," he threatened, "and I'm never going to speak to you again from this day." I didn't believe him, of course, but after that he only ever addressed me through my secretary. If he needed to tell me something, he would relay it directly to her, even though I was sitting right beside her in our office. On one occasion I interjected and said, "It's okay, Martin, the keys are in the top drawer of your desk." But he completely ignored me and went on giving my secretary the rest of the message for me. As a result I became extremely nervous of him, and because of the threat to get rid of me I began to wonder what he would do. I felt that I was being watched every single moment.'

Homing in on a particular weak point that Helen had expressed during her appointment interview, Martin changed her job role to include financial responsibilities which she had been assured would never arise because of her inexperience in this area. During the weeks that followed, training support was either cut short or never materialised. Tasks which were supposedly lined up for the following day failed to appear. Helen was then accused of not achieving what she had been asked to do. On one occasion, when she turned to her husband for help, he discovered she had been given a trick set of figures to tackle. Once her duties had changed beyond those of her original job description, she was destined to fail.

While Helen struggled to keep her head above water, Martin went on deriding her colleagues. The workplace was littered with bad language. Pete, a male colleague, known for his forthright approach, fed up with the bully's 'public-school crap', decided to complain to a higher authority about his attitude, his lack of manners and the constant flow of bad language. Instead of the hoped-for apology, it was *Pete* who was blamed for triggering the bad behaviour. Subsequently, he resigned from his £40,000 a year post. Pete had begun to realise that whenever he was with his wife, he was preoccupied with the stress he was experiencing at work. He valued his marriage, and was no longer prepared to suffer the effects of the persistent humiliation in front of junior staff, or Martin's inability to negotiate with others, convinced that his was always the right response.

Meanwhile, when Helen complained to personnel about her treatment, the response was totally unexpected. She was instructed *not* to use the confidential 'open-door' route to express her concerns to the managing director. 'You must never rise above your boss's head,' the personnel manager warned, reminding Helen that a year earlier she, too, had suffered a similar fate and had left the building in floods of tears on more than one occasion. 'I've had to work through it. You will, too,' was her only advice.

Three months later, it was Helen's turn to face what had become a familiar scenario in this particular organisation. Summoned to the boardroom one afternoon, she was told she was sacked. She was also instructed that she must be off the premises in fifteen minutes. Helen was informed that since her job had been changed, her work 'hadn't come up to scratch'. She had had no prior warning to this effect. Informing her that he was in a hurry, the senior colleague then slid a piece of paper towards her, explaining that her signature would secure the offer of three months' salary in lieu of notice, thereby relinquishing any further claims against the company. Helen's refusal met with a sharp retort: 'Don't be stupid about it. You know other people have tried. Your best bet is to take what is being offered. You don't have to tell anyone you've been fired, you can tell them we've made you redundant. Others have done that.' Helen, however, was not so easily swayed, and when the piece of paper remained on the table, unsigned, she was ordered not to leave the boardroom until a member of personnel arrived to accompany her back to her own office. Following three debriefing questions, which appeared to pose as a formal exit interview, she was literally frogmarched along the corridor to collect her personal belongings, and then escorted off the premises. As they reached the car, another male colleague demanded her keys so that he could search the inside. Nothing was removed, and whatever he was looking for remained a mystery.

Like those before her, Helen felt both hurt and ashamed by the experience of being sacked. In her view the action was unjustified. Now unemployed, she decided to seek the advice of a solicitor. Her account of happenings within her organisation convinced him that it was a clear-cut case for an industrial tribunal hearing for unfair dismissal.

The events which followed smacked of conspiracy. Helen's colleagues were instructed to make no contact with her. An anonymous letter was circulated within the company, ostensibly stating the real truth about her unexpected departure. 'Are you next?' it asked. 'Whatever happened to values of respect, integrity and openness? You are probably afraid to speak out. I am. But many of you know the truth.' The copies also referred to the bully's 'record of terror management' relating back to a previous employer. The letter was not only revealing, it was libellous. Although it was intended to offer Helen some support and draw attention to the plight of other colleagues who remained, Helen ended up being branded the originator of this letter. In the knowledge that she was entirely innocent, she made no objections when personnel informed her that the police would be calling to take her fingerprints, and those of her husband at his place of work. For three days she waited and although the telephone calls from personnel continued in an intimidating tone, the police never appeared.

Meanwhile, another director, who was scandalised by his company's treatment of Helen, also fell under suspicion and was accused by the managing director of writing the anonymous letter. When I contacted him at home one weekend, he was convinced that his telephone had been bugged. I did not hear from him again.

When I called the managing director to discuss his 'open-door' policy for the benefit of this book, I also drew his attention to the bullying that appeared to be going on within his organisation. He assured me that he would know if his people were experiencing such problems – not only through his regular and informal get-togethers with staff at different levels, but also through training sessions for which he was personally responsible. This conversation took place six days after Helen's sacking, and nine months after another colleague had also received a glowing annual appraisal from the managing director, only to face instant dismissal by Martin two weeks later.

None of it seemed to make sense, unless Martin was somehow blackmailing his boss. But now that Helen was tackling the decision to fire her directly, someone seemed determined that the reputation of the company must be protected at all costs. Was it, perhaps, fear of exposure if her case attracted press coverage at an industrial tribunal?

One Sunday, returning from an afternoon stroll, Helen and her husband noticed a company car parked across the road from their house. The keys to it lay on the front-door mat. Helen immediately felt unnerved. She clearly remembers her heart pounding as she peered from behind the living-room curtains towards nearby bushes, suddenly fearful that she might be under surveillance. Later, accompanied by her husband, she tried to drive the car away and return it to the leasing company, but after a few yards it stalled. An official inspection revealed that it had been sabotaged. Someone had clearly wanted it to stay where it was. And the leasing company reported that someone from Helen's office had telephoned the previous week, wanting to know whether the police would be involved if one of the company cars went missing.

Helen took one week to decide whether she had the courage to challenge both Martin and the organisation, purely on a matter of principle. She felt that she must, because what had happened both to her and to the others was wrong. It was a brave decision because it exposed her to the anxiety-ridden tactics of a company fearful that any link with bullying among its own ranks would damage its reputation as management troubleshooters, and therefore threaten its future as a financially viable concern.

Colleagues of Helen who voiced dismay at the injustice of her departure cut their own professional throats when they refused to back down. Moves to have her reinstated quickly foundered. One senior executive was dismissed without prior warning. Others followed.

In the end, however, the organisation's shoddy treatment of its own employees was never publicly exposed, because Helen's case was settled out of court. Wisely, she had kept all letters and documents relating to her previous employment, together with the taped messages from previous colleagues recorded on her answering machine

27

since her sacking. It was information her solicitor found invaluable.

In the absence of a reference, it was the copies of three annual appraisals, which she had also kept, that provided a valuable substitute. Within eight weeks of losing her job, Helen had been offered a manager's post elsewhere. On the advice of her solicitor, she decided to tell her new managing director that she had been sacked, and that a court hearing was on the horizon. His was a supportive response – not least because he frowned on the bullying he had encountered in three previous companies. But senior executives in the organisation which had sacked Helen chose to ignore information made available to them, even though it clearly identified Martin as an aggressor.

Helen's previous employers had access to a copy of a letter which had been sent to Martin by a fellow director in another company three years before. It criticised his 'attitude problem,' accused him of having a hit list and added:

'You give the impression that you think everyone else in the world is a dimwit and view problem areas with detached amusement and ridicule. This leads staff to the conclusion that this is a Board view, which in turn affects staff morale, and has a knock-on, domino-type destructive effect which could ultimately end in disaster. We, as directors, work as a team to achieve the company's fairly simple, well-defined corporate policies and objectives. If one player in that team decides he is going to play by different rules, to use different tactics, the teamwork breaks down.'

Even though the warning signs were there, and even though personal complaints were made about Martin's bullying behaviour, it was never challenged when he later changed jobs to join the senior ranks at the firm of management troubleshooters. Not surprisingly, his terror tactics continued unabated, and while he remained, fourteen men and women over a period of fourteen months were either sacked like Helen or resigned.

4
Bossy or Bully?

A sharp tongue is the only edged tool that grows keener with constant use.
Washington Irving, 'Rip Van Winkle'

No one would dispute that being in charge of others raises a difficult dilemma: 'How do I get the work done when the person simply doesn't seem to be doing the job properly? There isn't always time to sit back and say, "No, I won't push."'

These days, as organisations are more stretched to achieve greater efficiency, productivity and profit, the pressure is on every individual to come up to scratch. In the course of every working day, something is likely to happen which will test our reaction to others. Most of us are less than perfect when we are under pressure to achieve results, and occasionally people fly off the handle out of sheer frustration, or through their own response to feeling observed from above. The potential for one person nagging a subordinate to achieve the agreed objective could be considered a perfectly reasonable way of getting the job done. If it has not been carried out to a manager's exact specifications, however, is the person in charge entitled to snap? The question at issue here is: at what point does 'pushing' shade from legitimate and effective professionalism to punitive and counterproductive bullying? The distinction is crucially important, though clearly, in practice, it is all too easily glossed over or missed altogether when managers are themselves under pressure to perform.

30

Jean, a secretary describing her company director:

'His rule was that every letter had to be dealt with the day it arrived, yet if the work had been evenly spread over busy and slack days, it would have been better. Once he flung an envelope across the room at me, yelling at me to retype it. The name and address were correct in every respect, but I'd typed them about half an inch from where he wanted. Whenever he discovered the smallest error in my work, and even if the mistake was originally his fault, he would sit down, put his head in his hands and moan "No, no, no," or jump up and down shouting "It's wrong, it's wrong." In his case it seemed to be perfectionism gone mad, although he certainly got no pleasure from it. He seemed to be in a permanent state of agitation. If I couldn't find a paper in the files within a few seconds, it would be "Oh my God, oh my God, oh my God!" I was so anxious to please that every Monday morning I was in the office an hour early, and once, when I worked twelve hours without a break, I found him beside himself with rage next morning because he had found two small typing errors. How could I work well alongside this sort of attitude? The day I told him he was a bully, I was sacked.'

The Oxford Dictionary defines someone who is bossy as 'domineering'. The bully is described as 'a person using strength or power to coerce others by fear'. While neither is a particularly laudable character trait, a bossy person will usually acknowledge that this is the way they are if it is drawn to their attention. Being bossy is certainly aggressive, but this type of behaviour is generally short-lived and most people can learn to cope with it without too much difficulty in a working environment. To suggest otherwise would be to lay oneself open to a legitimate charge of, at best, 'wet idealism', and – if a manager is faced with people who are not pulling their weight, or being consistently late for work, or riding the waves until

31

retirement – of being downright unrealistic. 'Bossiness', however, turns to bullying when professional abrasiveness becomes tainted with an element of personal vindictiveness. Attempting to make people toe the line by singling them out, demeaning and devaluing them, is not an effective way of managing human beings.

Malcolm, a television director:

'Every day he would cause enormous stress to someone, shouting at them or attacking their efforts in front of others. At programme post-mortems there was never any constructive assessment. It was always an individual demolition job.

'Whatever he said could never be legitimately challenged without fear of recrimination. He seemed to know no other way of asserting himself than by being aggressive, and clearly felt he must be powerful enough to *over*power. What the bully does is make an example of a few to intimidate the rest until they fall into line. Hitler did the same.'

Val, an employee in a large high-street retail chain:

'He punished us by removing the radio from the staff room and turning the television screen to the wall so that we couldn't watch it during our lunch break. We were told that when the store's sales improved, the perks would be reinstated. His language would make a docker turn blue, and it was strongly suggested to us that we should forgo our lunch to help improve the takings for which he, not the staff, received a bonus.'

In a place of work, being a bully is about persistently snapping and finding fault. An employee who feels that they have the right to raise any concern and expect a considered response would be failed by any organisation which has a culture that endorses what it may perceive as a macho style of management. A bully is unlikely to listen to people's opinions and ideas, considers nothing and talks over others when they are trying to raise a point. The following quotes, incorporated in newspaper tributes following the death of a prominent business tycoon, illustrate a typical bullying style: 'He was frequently obnoxious to staff'; 'he was a hands-on person'; 'an employer who fired staff on a whim'; 'he never lost his almost childish thirst for attention'; 'his office was littered with people, waiting sometimes for hours for his attention'; 'he was a man with a booming voice dominating all around him'; 'he frequently gave people a public dressing down'.

In many cases, the bullying boss will not possess the social skills which equip a person with the art of compromise. One who has ruthlessly reached the top of his or her professional tree presents the most difficult problem for anyone in a personnel role. An extremely proficient captain of industry, for example, may make life hell for subordinates who don't respond in what he or she believes is the right way. If that person is a bully, there is unlikely to be any proper redress available to the individual who steps right into the line of fire.

A person in an ultimate position of power is unlikely to be successfully challenged. There is also an assumption in many organisations that the more senior you are, the less management training you need. After all, how could you possibly have reached that position if you didn't know precisely what being a boss was all about?

Most bullies, however, are wildly self-orientated. The way in which they see themselves will rarely tally with the view of those who are placed under attack. 'Telling the sod what to do' will be seen as perfectly justified in a leadership role. However, while occasional bossiness used to urge employees into action could be considered to have a constructive effect, the damning, condemnatory and often covert behaviour of an adult bully results in a wholly destructive outcome.

Given the task of differentiating between bossiness and bullying within the workforce is not as difficult as it may appear. Bossiness is unlikely to affect people's mental and physical health. In general, everyone is on the receiving end, and if the person becomes too overbearing, they can be challenged without fear of reprisal. Even a good moan among colleagues will relieve the tension, and at least everyone can confront it together.

Being bullied is an isolating experience. It tends not to be openly discussed in case this poses the risk of further ill-treatment. Those who are the prime targets often feel ashamed to discuss it with colleagues because their professional credibility is being called into question. The difficulty for the individual arises because bullying is swept under the all-embracing title of intimidation. What may be identified as the mildest form of intimidation is none the less very disturbing when you are the victim. As bullying moves up the Richter scale of aggression, and gets a severe grip on any group or individual, its physical effects are simply more severe.

Tackling the issue head on when a complaint *is* made means listening to two sides of the same story and looking for clues. The following accounts have been heard by a Director of Human Resources. He had to ask himself: Bossy or Bully?

Jenny, a political researcher with a newly appointed boss:

'On one occasion I was standing with a group of MPs when he started screaming at me that I was "a fucking cow". He uses four-letter words all the time, yelling insults down the phone. He is the person who has to sign my expenses, and I discovered he was phoning up every person I'd put on the claim form to check whether I really had taken them out to lunch and to find out what we had talked about. One of the politicians wrote to management and described him as rude and offensive, but all he got was a reprimand, so he just went on and did it again. Whenever he gets things wrong, he always takes it out on somebody else,

34

and he lies all the time. He doesn't trust anybody but himself.

'One of my female colleagues has become very distressed because she is always being left out of any activity. I know one man who has already left the company because all information was withheld from him so that he never knew what was happening. In the end he had a nervous breakdown because he felt so destroyed. At the moment my boss won't even talk to me because he knows I've complained. He's always telling me I'm incompetent, and on occasions I've felt absolutely insignificant. Now, if I think I'm going to see him, I get collywobbles in my stomach and I feel sick. I suffer such stress because of this man that I have to stay at home until I can face going to work again. I get terrible indigestion, and for the past six months I've experienced panic attacks when I'm in the office. Colleagues tell me it's very frightening because I go bright red in the face and find it difficult to breathe.'

On the strength of these allegations, the Director of Human Resources held several meetings with the man concerned, and recounts the alleged bully's analysis of his own behaviour:

'He would deny that it was bullying for a start. He believes that this trait in him is a manifestation of the high level of professionalism he brings to the job. What others perceive as bullying is seen by him as a short fuse; that it's his way of solving problems in certain situations to get the job done. He is someone who can be perfectly normal, calm and controlled, but then unleash verbal aggression with a disregard for the problems this appears to create. He has been very open to me in admitting that he has this defect in his character, although he rationalises it by saying that it does help him maintain very high standards in his own

35

work. In his mind, the destructive element of his behaviour is outweighed by the productive effect of what is professionally achieved. He also says, "It isn't all me. I'm pushed into this situation because she's not that good at her job." In other words, "She is finding things to complain about to excuse her own incompetence, and because of her weaknesses, she is seeing bullying when it isn't there." He is rather proud of what you might call a sergeant major reputation; the sort of person who knows what he's doing and, in order to reach a particular goal, believes that people need to be told exactly how to do things and put in their place. When the pressure is off him, and he's not in a work environment, he is a very nice, humorous, pleasant person.'

Presented with the facts by these two individuals, and a representative from the National Union of Journalists, the Director of Human Resources concluded that the accused was behaving like a bully. Faced with the prospect of disciplinary procedure, this man elected to take early retirement. He has since taken up a public relations post with another organisation.

Because the truth in situations like the above often needs to be gleaned, more vigilance is required of those responsible for the mental and financial health of any organisation. While a person who is being bossy is unlikely to be tolerated indefinitely, bullying, when it takes place at work, is so full of complexities that it can be too intangible to be identified by the individual alone. One thing is certain – a person who is being bullied will not be working to the best of their ability, nor will they be co-operating as well as they should within a team. These are important clues.

It is rarely just one person who is on the receiving end, so it is likely that the performance of a whole group will alter. When a new boss takes up an appointment, a decline in overall standards should be seen as a warning sign. It should be an indication that the situation is worth investigating when those who could be relied on in the past start making mistakes.

In the next chapter, six men and women reveal what happened to them when they experienced the effects of bullying at work and their plight was ignored despite the fact that all the warning signs were there.

In the first of these accounts, one of a group of eight men who was being bullied finally found the appropriate language with which to make a complaint. For anyone who knew what to look for, the visible effects on these people should have set off alarm bells. For the personnel director involved, recognition came too late. Here she describes what she eventually acknowledged as the effects of persistent bullying:

'One was very gaunt, red-eyed and unshaven. He seemed to have lost any pride in the way he looked. He was working very, very ineffectively and he appeared frightened. Another one of them constantly chain-smoked and seemed to have the shakes. A third was pale and withdrawn and seemed very uptight. When I told the bullying lecturer this was how these men had looked when I met them in my office, he said, "Yes, I think they must lead a very wild life." When I put it to him that it was my belief his behaviour had been responsible for their appearance, he said, "That's ridiculous!" All of us involved in representing him concluded that he was such an insensitive person he was totally unconscious of the effect his behaviour was having. I saw him as the sort of person who, in wartime, would be taken on as a concentration camp commandant.'

5
The Bullied

'I'd lie in bed feeling so angry
I just wanted to kill him'

Nick, aged forty, loved his work as a technician in a large academic establishment, convinced that he couldn't have so much fun anywhere else and still get paid for it. He arrived for work at least an hour early every morning because he simply liked being there, even after fourteen years on the same site. He particularly enjoyed the responsibility of advising students and running a workshop. Three months after a highly respected lecturer was appointed as his new boss, Nick could barely drag himself out of bed in the mornings because he felt so professionally demolished. When he complained about his treatment to union colleagues, his own macho image, and a reputation for being outspoken, meant that no one was prepared to take him seriously . . .

'It was a gradual wearing-down process, mostly by subtle means. The new boss removed every area of my responsibility, excluding me from any planning decisions and undermining everything I said or did. As technicians, our main task is to offer advice to students while they're working, but this wasn't allowed. They had to be referred straight to him if they wanted to make something, and no one was allowed to do anything that didn't conform to his rigid style. In his opinion there was no one else in the country better than him at what he did, and his was indisputably the only opinion. When he was addressing John, the guy who worked under me, he never used his name, just derisory nicknames like "oddball" and "oppo". John's degree meant nothing to this man. He shouted at him all the time and showed him absolutely no respect. After a month John wanted to leave, but I told him it would get better, that we just had to prove to this guy that we were really good at our jobs. In fact it got worse and worse.

'When I got back from a foreign exchange, I found he had completely rearranged my workshop. He relegated us to trivial jobs all the time, dragging stuff out of the rubbish skips and ordering us to take out all the nails and screws just to save 10 pence. He would keep me waiting for weeks before he'd agree to sign an order form for some new tool, by which time the job had been done. It could have been done in half the time with the right equipment. After a while, what had been the busiest area in our department was down to half a dozen students a year. No one wanted to get involved, and most of the students were frightened of him, too. Many people feared this man, even some of his fellow academics. There were others who appeared to be pally with him, although that was probably their way of trying to avoid any aggro. Sometimes he would be quite nice, but within an hour he'd swing the other way and we'd only have to hear his voice outside the door for everybody to go quiet. People were all the time glancing over their shoulders with dread, in case he suddenly appeared and started having a go at them again. In three years he said good morning to me twice, and the nearest I got to praise was when he took charge of a plan of mine that I'd carefully put together and stole the credit for it, passing it off as his own idea. As far as he was concerned, technicians were nothing more than glorified cleaners, and by ignoring us, he didn't have to acknowledge that we existed.

'After three months of this I told everybody I could that this was what he was doing, but when I recounted some of the incidents at a union meeting, there was raucous laughter and I was told not to be so silly. No one took me seriously, and after I told a senior colleague that this man was making my life hell, he said that his understanding of him was as a really professional person, and that if I was being treated like this, it must be because of something I'd done. Eventually, our boss nearly destroyed him, too.

'Long before that, what was happening at work dominated conversations with girlfriends and I became a seriously heavy smoker. For twenty-four hours a day, seven days a week, I felt completely stressed out. I'd be thinking about it at weekends, on holidays abroad – it never left me. My stomach was in a knot most of the time. His mere presence made me a bag of nerves, and if I knew he had a bee in his bonnet about something, I'd feel as if the blood was literally draining out of my legs when he approached. He had destroyed my self-confidence, and for three years I know I worked badly because I was both so stressed, and so frustrated at not being able to fulfil my usual role. I began to sleep very badly. I'd lie there feeling so angry and so impotent. I just wanted to kill him. I was brought up to stand up to bullies, without the use of violence, and because I believe in getting on with people, I tried really hard with him. When I told him I thought the situation was ridiculous and that we must get the problem sorted out, he said, "What problem?" I explained that it was the way he didn't talk to me. "I talk to you all I need to," came his cutting reply.

'It reached the point when the eight of us he was bullying on a regular basis considered getting him beaten up just to get him off our backs. I did feel that I had stood up for what I believed in, but I hadn't really. I mostly told him what he wanted to hear, and

40

I'd say yes to anything in the end, just for a quiet life. If I was asked to clean the floor, John would say to me, "You're not paid to do it, how can you demean yourself like this?" Then he'd look at me as if I was some sort of dog that had been told off. The turning point came when I heard other people talking about their experiences on the radio. After that I was able to explain to the union executive that I needed help because I was being bullied. I felt very resentful towards the organisation for allowing it to happen. In the end, the most important thing for me was finally being believed.'

Anna, one of the two National Association of Local Government Officers (NALGO) representatives who handled the official complaint eventually made by the eight technicians, was shocked by 'their level of paranoia' which became evident through their level of mistrust:

'As we got out of the car, Nick appeared round a corner, hissing at us to follow him, and gesturing with his finger that his boss was on site. We were silently led down a corridor to the workshop, where people were being furtively called on the telephone to come on down. It seemed like some huge conspiracy. When we moved on to the lecture room, everyone was still creeping about, looking over their shoulders and reassuring each other that they would be all right, shutting all the doors at the same time. They looked a sorry lot, slouched in their chairs with their cigarettes, telling me how they used to really enjoy their jobs. These days it was off to the pub every night to get plastered and try to forget what had happened during the day. People who had anything to do with this man used to dread meeting him in the corridor, and they would stand there, with butterflies in their stomachs, bracing themselves for whatever was coming. As I sat down at the word processor to type out an official letter of complaint to personnel, one of them stood over me to shield the screen in case anyone walked in. Another guarded the printer, and great care was taken immediately afterwards to erase the file in case it was discovered by the man they so feared. It set the adrenalin going, and I was even beginning to feel the fear for myself. At one stage I thought: this is so weird.'

Following an internal investigation, the senior lecturer was due to face a disciplinary charge of gross misconduct when he suddenly resigned. A few months later he took up a new post at another academic establishment. Nick remained in his job, but owing to the effects of the bullying, several of his colleagues decided to leave. In Chapter 10 you can follow the individual dilemmas of the unions involved, as well as that of the personnel department, in dealing for the first time with a case of bullying at work.

'She even kept a daily record of how often you'd been to the ladies' and threatened to deduct the time used up from your pay'

Jackie was eighteen. It was her first job. By joining the Regional Health Authority as a clerical officer, she was upholding a family tradition. Both her parents were well known for their long service in the same organisation, and Jackie's academic record had already identified her as someone with good promotion prospects.

'When I first started I did notice how our supervisor continually picked on one of the other nine girls, embarrassing her in front of everyone by calling her stupid names in a really sarcastic way. I just assumed it was a personality clash, but when the girl talked to me about how it upset her, she pointed out that the woman considered it the fate of one girl at a time to be bullied. The day this girl got a transfer she told me "You'll be next", and I was. Almost within hours the supervisor accused me of not doing my work properly, constantly rubbishing whatever I did. No one but her was ever right, and even if you knew you were, and could prove it, she'd say, "I'm telling you *I'm* right and that's the way it is." There were hundreds of envelopes to send out every day, but if I didn't get the frank absolutely straight, she would call me a useless bitch and accuse me of wasting another envelope. After the other girls told me that she frequently checked my flexicard, I'd find it scored right through. Then she would claim that I'd left a few minutes early, even though this was always untrue. Most of the time she marched into the office, shouting like a sergeant major, and stood by the loo door, commanding anyone who appeared to "get back in the office". She even kept a daily record of how often you'd been to the Ladies' and threatened to deduct the time used up from your pay. On one occasion she informed me that I'd been in there for precisely six minutes and thirty-three seconds. Because she managed through fear, everybody kept quiet, and when I decided to complain to personnel about the way she behaved, I was told I was overreacting. (It was only later that I discovered that the supervisor and the personnel officer were good friends.) If I made any sort of a scene I was labelled a troublemaker.

'During the time I was there, the Health Authority were enabling me to carry on with my further education, but this became increasingly difficult. If I got my books out during a lunch break, she would say, "That is what you do at home. I'm not allowing people to study in here when this office is open all day." I used to end up sitting down to my studies well past midnight, once I'd done all the household chores, and then get very overtired. When I did eventually get to bed, I didn't sleep well because my brain would be

43

going over what had happened during the day. I also felt intense frustration because I couldn't get back at her and I didn't know what to do. I was scared most of the time, for the whole two years, but I was living away from home and if I'd walked out, I wouldn't have been able to pay the rent. Around this time I made frequent visits to the surgery with stress-related complaints, but the migraines were the worst. I had a dreadful headache for most of the day, and knowing that when I got to work there were going to be problems, I also lost weight. At one time I became so run down that I ended up with flu and was off work for two weeks. When I returned, one of the older women in the office warned me that the supervisor had been putting about a really vicious rumour that I was pregnant, and that was why I'd been away. I was about to put in for promotion, so any suggestion of scandal could have ruined my chances. As it was, I later learnt that she had already refused any recommendation because she was backing a friend for the post instead. When I heard what she'd been saying I was extremely angry, so I cornered her behind a filing cabinet, told her she was a really evil woman, and threatened to sue her for sexual slander concerning the pregnancy rumour, unless I received a written apology. She was persuaded to apologise, but it made things worse because she picked on me even more after that.

'I'm convinced that she enjoyed the power, and that she saw it as her right to treat people in this way just because she was in charge. But because of her I got so low and miserable that I absolutely hated going into the office. When I was there I'd volunteer for any other little jobs that would get me out of the way for a while, but at the end of the day I used to think: I can't cope with this, and go home and cry my eyes out. I just lived for her holidays. When she wasn't there the atmosphere was transformed. It was much more friendly because people felt at ease. They even talked to me, which most of them didn't do the rest of the time in case she started to bully them, too. I finally got my promotion, and the day I was leaving I challenged this woman about her appalling treatment. I was met with an emphatic denial.'

Jackie went on to achieve her BTEC National Diploma, with five distinctions, and continued up the promotional ladder. Several years later, after her supervisor had been made redundant, she met her again in the street and confronted her about the treatment she had meted out at the time. 'I was under pressure,' she replied, with increasing volume. 'And you have got to realise that you young girls needed bringing into line . . .'

'She could be very affable and helpful, but then suddenly she would start to humiliate you, so you never knew where you were'

At twenty-two, Angela was an English graduate about to start her first job in an employment agency:

'At first I was keen and excited, although I must confess that I was also a little scared that I might not be able to do what was asked of me. My immediate boss didn't help matters. She was a middle-aged executive with huge eyes which she would fix on one person at a time and just glare.

'It was very intimidating. If I questioned something she had asked me to type she would tell me how stupid and inadequate I was in front of the whole department. In certain letters she kept wanting to use the phrase "extenuating circumstances", but if I pointed out that this wasn't appropriate, she became very angry and would screech at me: "Who do you think you are?" Sometimes mistakes were made and that person would get a public dressing-down so that

45

everyone in the room would be aware of "their misdemeanour". If people asked for a day's leave, often for really quite important reasons, she'd give a curt refusal without any reason whatsoever. When it happened to me I felt I should have said "Stuff you, it's my leave", but I was twenty-two and very inexperienced. Most days there was trouble of some kind, but as it was my first job, I assumed to start with that this was quite normal.

'Most of my colleagues had been under her thumb too long to complain, so the atmosphere was very unhappy and downcast. She went out of her way to discredit each of us in turn, always in front of everyone else, but I don't think the people at the top realised what she was like because they never saw her at her worst. Her immediate superiors appeared to be just as scared as we were. Whenever she'd had a go at me personally, I'd go into the toilet for half an hour, have a cry, and then come back and carry on. None of us talked about it to each other. We were too afraid of attracting more trouble. Sometimes she could be very affable and helpful, but then suddenly she would start to humiliate you, so you never knew where you were. I felt battered by her personality, as if there was no room in the world for the rest of us.

'After a time she began to tell me I was "abnormal" and "disturbed", especially if I tried to express an opinion. At one time I felt defiant and thought: No, damn it, I *am* right, but I was paranoid by then, and even though I stood up to her when no one had in the past, I began to sit there and take it like everyone else. When I started to suffer from infections and rashes, my doctor insisted that I paid him a monthly visit to talk about the problems at work. I had begun to feel so unworthy and so inadequate that when she came into the room I'd literally go white and shake. Even when she knew my father had died, and my mother was

46

diagnosed terminally ill, her behaviour towards me didn't change.

'At home I didn't want to go out or do anything other than talk about what was happening at work. I used to love writing, but it stilted the creative side of me, and at the end of the day I was so exhausted, all I wanted to do was sit and stare at the television. The depression which gripped me after a while nearly broke up my marriage. At work people went on making desperate attempts to try for other jobs outside the department, but we all depended on her recommendation. It was a standing joke that the only way out was if you were pregnant or dead. Eventually I did get promoted to another department, but even then I was still frightened that I'd see her again. Looking back, I wish I'd thrown all the books on the floor and left, but it was my first job and I was worried about a reference . . .'

Two years later Angela left her job, shortly before the birth of her first child, and resolved never to work in an office again. She is now a teacher in further education and a published writer.

'From the moment I arrived in the office on Monday morning it was like going into a cage with an unpredictable animal'

When Fran, aged forty-one, returned from maternity leave to her old job on a daily provincial newspaper, the new editor had been in place for one week. Despite an established reputation as a skilled features writer, her professional ability was immediately called into question. After twenty years in journalism she was reduced to relatively menial tasks usually reserved for trainee reporters. This marked the beginning of what her husband describes as 'a clinical reign of terror' which drove most of her twenty-eight colleagues out of their jobs.

'The atmosphere at work had become quiet and hostile. We were discouraged from chatting and having the usual office banter – in fact there was practically a no-talking rule. Even on the telephone we were not expected to spend any time establishing any sort of rapport with the public. I had come back to work expecting reasonable status as a writer, but not only was I assigned to jobs like golden weddings and press releases, I was put under someone fifteen years younger who wasn't even properly qualified.

'Initially I felt insulted, but when I asked to see the editor, he told me he was under no obligation to honour any previous agreement. "We're doing things my way now," he said, "and you will do as you are told." He was very difficult to confront because he used to remove himself from the office, and when he was there, he was surrounded by people who sided with him.

'As the pressure built up, I could see other reporters looking strained and upset, but I didn't know why because nobody said anything. Those who were picked on and humiliated in public very quickly got out. Then I received the first of many memos, which would sometimes run to two pages of A4 paper, criticising the standard of my work and pointing out that my stories were having to be knocked back and rewritten. In all my experience, under three previous editors, this had never happened, and when I read that first memo I literally had a physical reaction. I was sweating, my scalp prickled, and I had this feeling that the whole office was staring at me. The memo made it clear that copies had gone to six other senior members of staff, so I was terribly shaken, but I didn't tell anyone because it was embarrassing. I think it was a bit like a woman who's been raped not telling the police in case they think it was her fault.

'It was more than a year later before I became aware that others had received memos like this too.

The editor's secretary was comforting me in the ladies' loo after I'd fainted when she told me how badly she'd felt about having to type them. Those memos were obviously designed to intimidate from the outset, and they succeeded. It was the power of suggestion: setting somebody up to worry about something. The news editor would go over them with me in detail, as if I had behaved like a naughty schoolgirl. At the time, each of us thought we were the only one because nobody told, nobody stood up and waved them about. They upset me so much that I couldn't even bear to put them at the back of a drawer, or even in a dustbin, because that meant that they not only still existed, they would go on festering. Instead, I burnt them. Looking back, that was wrong. It meant I had no evidence, and that was a mistake.

'As I went on getting copy thrown back at me, I began to think it was all my fault. If someone repeatedly questions anything you do, whether it's answering the telephone or writing the word July, after a while you begin to wonder whether you *are* doing it right, especially if no one else is *telling* you that you are. No one was, of course, because it was happening to them, too. One correspondent became so overloaded on top of all his specialist work that it was quite ludicrous, but when he complained to the editor, he was told not to carp. Everything I did was repeatedly criticised, and even if I wrote an intro to a story exactly as I'd been instructed, a sub-editor would come over to me later and say, "Why have you written it this way, surely this is the obvious angle?" Then I'd have to redo it. It was very undermining, especially when the editor was sitting in the middle of the room while all this was going on, swivelling in his seat and fixing me with a stare. Whatever I did seemed to be wrong. On one occasion, I drove a few miles from the office to cover a story which needed a personal interview, and was later accused of incurring unnecessary mileage. Another time I collected a quote over the telephone and was promptly told off for not doing the thirty-mile round trip to collect some personal quotes. Time and time again it seemed as if I was being set up to get it all wrong.

'Other people were publicly dressed down for things they genuinely hadn't done, and at the end of each week the editor would go over our copy, word by word, inch by inch, to assess the quality and quantity. Interviews in the front office were timed, and most of us felt under constant pressure to produce something or come under attack. I can remember frantically rummaging through drawers in search of press releases to rewrite so that I wouldn't be accused of sitting there twiddling my thumbs. I became desperate to be occupied all day long, simply to stay out of trouble. From the moment I arrived in the office on Monday morning, it was like being in a cage with an unpredictable animal. I used to go to work in a state of dread, wondering if it would be my turn to be verbally done over.

'There were many days when nothing would happen, then out of the blue something would come, and at first you just didn't know why you'd been hit. After that you'd be repeatedly hit for some days, and then it would stop again. As a result I became more and more distressed and miserable. I cried a lot at home, shouting and screaming at the kids. I'd yell at them to clear out of my sight and tell them it was all too much for me. I felt totally defeated, and to a certain extent I conveyed the blame on to the children. Physically I became worn out. My menstrual cycle went haywire, and because I was tired and dejected, it put stress on my marital relationship. I just didn't want to *know* my partner. Whenever he put it to me that I should confront what was happening at work, I'd burst into tears and tell him he didn't understand. I'd worked for bastards before, but they always had some redeeming qualities, and if there was any kind of ding-dong, I knew I was up to it so it never made me lose any sleep. But this was insidious, and all the time there was the expectation that a trap was being laid for you. Once people started to leave, there was a general feeling that senior management would notice that good journalists were pouring down the drain and wonder why. Then we began to realise that the salary bill must be a fraction of what it had been, so perhaps they liked it like this. Even so, the paper's circulation had dropped dramatically, so we'd still think: It can't go on for ever, someone is bound to put a stop to it. But it didn't stop, of course, and here I was, a one-time union official, without the strength even to put pen to paper to make a complaint. I knew that if I approached my union, I'd have to make allegations to support my case at an industrial tribunal, and that meant further confrontation. I knew I couldn't cope. I didn't want to leave because I'd always loved local journalism, and in that area there were no other jobs around for journalists.

'The people who could escape were those with no responsibilities. Those of us with mortgages and young children were trapped. In the end, my health suffered so much that after thirteen months I decided to leave. As soon as I knew I wasn't going back I felt personally released. My health improved in leaps and bounds over the following weeks, and relationships at home relaxed. Then the hating started and I thought: You bastard, you did this to me, and if you hadn't I could still be working. While I was being bullied I firmly believed that I had been a sponge on the whole establishment; that I'd been useless from the outset; that I had no worth to anybody at all. One day I found a couple of old cuttings and I thought: I *used* to be good. I'm not any more, but I actually was once. Before I left that job I didn't believe I'd ever been any good. My confidence in my own ability was so shattered that I didn't believe I'd ever be able to work again.'

Fran now works as a freelance journalist. She was encouraged by a professional colleague to pursue a story which merited her specialist skill, and in spite of some initial wavering, she was persuaded to offer it to the features department at *The Independent*. She says: 'I couldn't believe it! I got a warm, positive response, and people were not only nice to me, they actually liked what I wrote.'

'At one time I even contemplated putting a bomb under her car, just to get her to stop. Suicide would have been a blessed release'

Bill, a teacher in his fifties, was well known for building a special rapport with pupils. He preferred not to adhere to a structured syllabus, and despite his unconventional and rather eccentric approach, his classes achieved good academic grades. Bill was admired by both parents and pupils for his ability to communicate his enthusiasm for science, and he had a faithful following. When he changed jobs, he was academically better qualified than his head of department, but she was a highly organised teacher, and by the end of the first term she was accusing him of being poorly trained, innumerate and inadequate.

'I soon realised that she demanded a much more specific teaching programme that must be planned well in advance, and basically I didn't know where I was, so in one respect she was right. We had totally different styles, which the Education Authority must have been well aware of, so coping with me at the start must have tripled her workload. The remedies she set out for me made me feel about as confident as a kid being given detention by his teacher, but I devoted hours and hours every evening to planning classes and making teaching notes, desperately trying to adapt to her style. Whatever I did was still wrong, and if I argued with her it was impossible to convince her that I might have a point worth considering. She always made herself out to be five hundred per cent right, and at staff meetings she would stand up and ask why other people couldn't do things the way they did them in her department, where everything was "so wonderfully innovative". She never made space for other people's ideas.

'Generally speaking she was greatly disliked, and I eventually lost count of the number of times I saw pupils coming out of her department in tears. She frequently shouted me down for whatever I did, and I could see colleagues thinking: Oh God, she's going to have another go at him. As far as she was concerned, my appointment was a mistake because it was like trying to fit a square peg into a round hole. I went on and on, working into the early hours to try to fit in with her requirements, but all I ever got was a constant barrage of criticism, and I became so nervous of getting it wrong again, I just went on making mistakes. I'd receive criticisms covering two sides of A4 telling me what was wrong, which appeared to be everything. When I challenged some of her comments she'd say, "While you're here, Bill, you'll do things my way or not at all." She was totally inflexible. If I was called into her office she would slate me for anything and everything, narrowing her eyes and thrusting her body towards me in a very threatening fashion. I'd stand there, trying to make a point, but she never gave me so much as a millisecond to get out an appropriate response. Every encounter became so intimidating that it reduced me to schoolboy level, scuttling through corridors and trying to sneak past her door in case I got into more trouble.

'Because I was working till I practically dropped every evening, I gradually became worn out and overstressed. People in other departments were assuring me that what was happening wasn't my fault, but I was full of self-doubt, and the belief that as a grown man I ought to be able to cope with whatever was flung at me. It struck me that as I was not coping with it, I must be a real wimp. Whenever she was present, I was always excluded from social conversation, although she was always demanding to know what I was doing, so I became totally demoralised. I tried to be optimistic and think: Well, this week I'll get it right, things will improve, but they never did. I felt spied on all the time, and because the atmosphere was so horrendous, I went on underperforming and making mistakes. Every Sunday night I would think: Oh God, it's going to start all over again. I'd have butterflies in my stomach on the way to school, and the moment I got there I'd have diarrhoea. At lunchtimes I would aim for a table occupied by friends, preferably with no other spare places so there wasn't any chance of my head of department sitting down and having another go at me. Afterwards, I'd get in the car and drive round the corner and spend the rest of the time reading a book, just to stay out of her way and avoid another verbal lashing. Two or three nights a week I'd wake up in a fury with my teeth clenched, feeling murderous. I really wanted to knock that woman to the ground and jump all over her, or ring her up in the middle of the night just to disturb her sleep. At one time I even contemplated putting a bomb under her car, just to get her to stop. Suicide would have been a blessed release, and it did pass through my mind, because then I would have been out of it. What stopped me was the thought of what it would do to my family, and I had already caused them enough misery by ceasing to communicate.

'When my head of department decided to check up on my lessons, I was like a gibbering wreck. My knees went to jelly and my hands trembled, so when she chipped in from the back of the classroom with a seemingly abstract question, I was so terrified, I couldn't think what the hell she was talking about. With hindsight, it was a perfectly simple question that I could have answered immediately, but I simply seized up. I'd never met anyone who affected me in this way, except as a small boy. There was another occasion when she got up, grabbed the chalk and just took over. Afterwards, some of the GCSE kids said things like "She doesn't like you, does she, sir?" and "She's not very nice to you, is she?" At other times she'd start laying into me before the kids had even left the classroom. It was the only time in my entire teaching career that my pupils' grades weren't so good. When she wasn't actually in my classroom, the door to her office a few feet away would be left open so that she could listen. If I managed to push it shut, it would be opened again. Sometimes I'd see her peering through the glass to see what was written on the blackboard. My state of anxiety was such that the doctor prescribed prolonged sick leave, and when I pressed my union for a transfer, they told me they'd tried this tactic in the past and in their experience it didn't work. It was always the teacher's ability that was blamed rather than the appointment itself.

'When I complained about this woman to an official in the Education Authority, he told me not to let her win. The head of the school took the same tack. Only colleagues were supportive. Some of them were even praying for me at one point, in spite of the fact that I must have been a real pain in the arse to cope with. In desperation my wife gave me a miniature tape-recording machine for my birthday so that I could stick it in my jacket pocket and record the vicious exchanges with my head of department. Listening to those recordings is still upsetting. In the end I didn't know who to turn to. I was fed up with constantly waiting for the Sword of Damocles to fall, so I took my

55

union's advice and resigned through ill health. After twenty years as a teacher, I felt I'd been forced out of a job I had previously loved.'

Bill's reluctant decision meant a drop in income from £1,000 to £400 a month, with five years on his mortgage still to pay. He wrote dozens of applications for jobs outside the teaching profession, but he was up against the mass pruning of employees during a recession. He finally resorted to door-to-door sales to help pay the household bills.

When a person is being bullied at work, family life is likely to become equally stressed . . .

After thirty years of marriage to Bill, the teacher in the previous story, Wendy watched her relationship being severely eroded as the effects of bullying took over their lives.

'Bill gradually became quiet and withdrawn, and although I knew it had to be something to do with work, whenever I tried to make him talk about it, he became very irritable. He lost weight, too, and looked very white, with these terrible bags under his eyes. I began to think he'd been to see our GP, who'd told him there was something seriously wrong that he wasn't telling me. Emotionally he lost interest in everything, and he would sleep for hours on end. Some days I'd even find him alseep half an hour after we'd got up. I couldn't understand it. In his previous job he'd always come home drained, but happily tired, and he couldn't wait to get back there the following day. I was so petrified that there was something seriously wrong that I watched every single thing he did. If he put his head in his hands at the dining-table I'd say, "What's the matter, what's all this?" and he'd say, "For God's sake leave me alone." Eventually he

56

did tell me what was happening at work, then he ceased to communicate at all. He was working such long hours in the evening that there was no time for any social life. There was certainly no time or energy for sex, because every waking moment was work.

'For three years there was no laughter in our house. The bullying had a terrible effect on us both, because it also made me very angry that he could allow it to happen. I just couldn't understand how he could let someone wipe the floor with him, and I remember thinking: You're an idiot, how the hell can I ever respect you? You're not a man, you're a wimp. As a result we totally grew apart, both physically and emotionally. When we weren't snapping at each other, there were long silences. I began to suffer from high blood pressure and there was this awful buzzing in my ears. Even our married daughter became anxious. She would telephone from the other side of the country every evening and talk about all sorts of little things you knew she could cope with. Then she'd say, "How's Daddy? Can I talk to him?" It was as if she wanted to be certain that he wasn't dead. Because I had chosen to remain a housewife and hide behind his degrees, when he felt threatened, I suddenly felt inadequate, as if it was my professional competence that was being challenged. I also felt very lost and lonely, but I really resented him for getting himself into this fix, and I got to the point of wanting to walk out. The pressure on him at work brought out the most terrible things in us both, but I knew I couldn't do anything about it. I knew I had to watch while he tried to fight his way through this immovable human being. What concerned me most was at what cost to his health and mine, and to the marriage.

'Our friends were out of their minds with worry, and sometimes they'd stop me in the street and ask what effect it was having on me. I'd tell them I was fine, of course, but what I really wanted to say was,

"Hold me, just hold me, and for God's sake do something!" Eventually I did take a job, just to get me out of the house, because home was a constant reminder of what was wrong. Ironically, for me, work was the only place where I felt safe. At one time I realised that I was happiest when Bill's boss was being horrible to him. I knew then that it couldn't get any worse, so at least I knew where I was. Bill has always been very even-tempered, and slow to flare, but I worried that if this woman pushed him much further he'd become physically violent, and then he wouldn't be able to stop, he'd kill her. It would have been kinder if she'd hit him on the head with a hammer and dealt with him quickly and cleanly.

'I felt as if I'd like to hide behind a wall and pelt rotten apples at those in the organisation who had allowed this to happen. It made me so helpless, it reduced me to petty, childlike behaviour. It reached the point where I'd see people in cars doing ordinary things like going shopping and I'd wonder if *they'd* ever gone through anything like this. Then I'd think: I hope to God they never do, because I know what it does.'

Nine months after Bill resigned, he and Wendy were beginning to talk to each other again. After the most stressful period in a previously happy marriage, humour was creeping back into their lives for the first time in three years. Wendy has become more self-reliant.

HELPING YOURSELF

Perhaps the most common – and doubtless well-meaning – piece of advice given to those being bullied is confrontation. Unfortunately, this apparently straightforward and common-sense approach is more likely to enrage than to persuade the person to see reason. It will almost certainly result in an increased vindictiveness towards whoever is making the accusation. Confrontation is too unsafe an approach to be made by the individual alone, unless direct opposition to this style of behaviour is established at a very early stage using a firm tone of voice.

The next section of this book is designed to help you realise that whether they are aware of the fact or not, bullies are themselves victims on the run. The risk in challenging their behaviour is that it not only forces them to face what they are running from, it gets in the way of their complex struggle for power and personal security.

Whether you have been singled out or not, there can be equally complicated reasons why you, as an individual, will be ill-equipped to try to get the bully off your back.

Help for both the bully and the bullied can be provided by the organisation in which both work (see Chapters 10–12). Before any action can be taken, you, as the individual being bullied, have to be aware of what is going wrong. Personal survival is about recognising what is happening to you while you are still only slightly affected.

Early warning signs

- This working relationship feels different to any I have previously experienced.
- I am being persistently got at.
- My work is being criticised, even though I know my standards haven't slipped.
- I am beginning to question whether these mistakes I am supposed to have made really are my fault.

If this is an accurate picture of what is happening to you at work, reflect on what has happened in the recent past and ask yourself: If everything was all right before, why not now?

- What has changed?
- Do you have a new boss?
- Has pressure on your current boss increased?
- Have you recently changed jobs?
- Are your objectives being repeatedly altered?
- Have you been asked to do things outside your job description?
- Are you under more personal scrutiny?
- Are you feeling less involved?

Something about you may make the bully feel threatened. To remove that threat, it may be their intention – conscious or otherwise – to get rid of you. For example, they may give you tasks you are unlikely to achieve. The bully will be looking for any reason to accuse you of poor performance which could lead to eventual dismissal. It is essential that you maintain your self-respect at this stage.

Initial tactics worth trying

Stand firm if you come under verbal attack. Tell the bully that you will not tolerate personal remarks.

Remember that this type of person is likely to be at their worst when they feel under pressure.

Remain confident in your own judgement and ability.

If you clash over work contributions, keep calm and say what has to be said quietly and coherently.

If objectives or instructions are unclear, ask for written clarification. Explain that this will provide an *aide-mémoire* to help you achieve the aims within the given time. If things do not improve, you already have important evidence.

A better understanding of the reasons for a bully's aggressive behaviour (see Chapter 6) will help you know what you are up against.

Asserting yourself

Check with previous appraisals or annual reports to confirm that it is not *your* performance that has altered. Ask colleagues for their assessment.

Check your job description. Make sure it is not being abused.

Retain copies of all correspondence, including memos, relating to your job.

Keep a detailed, dated record of every verbal attack and every new instruction.

Check your staff handbook or policy booklet – if these are available – to establish what you can do if you feel you are being bullied and the time has come to make a complaint.

Before you decide to fight back through official channels, it is worth considering an informal approach. First of all, however, see if any of your colleagues look tense or troubled. Bullying at work usually affects several members of staff at any one time. The more people experiencing the same type of conduct, the less likely any complaint will be thought of as a personality clash on your part.

Other practical steps

- Ask a trade-union representative, or a personnel or welfare officer, to inform the bully why people at work find his or her behaviour aggressive, and to point out the effect it is having. If this proves ineffective, ask them to put it in writing, to the bully and the bully's boss as appropriate.
- Avoid being alone with the bully. Wherever possible, insist on a witness being present at any meeting which is likely to be behind closed doors.
- Send a confidential memo to senior management above your boss, informing them that you are being bullied, and by whom. Make it clear that you trust this will not be allowed to continue. Point out that if it is stopped, you and your colleagues will be able to get on with your work, and the organisation's output will cease to be affected. If there is no improvement, repeat the process. Keep copies.
- If, as a group of individuals, you realise that bullying is the source of your distress, contact ACAS – the Advisory, Conciliation and Arbitration Service (addresses at the back of this book). Tell them there is a problem with industrial relations in your company, school or organisation, and if the evidence is available they may be able to investigate and provide help. ACAS also offers guidance for employers in need of advice.

It may be, of course, that without realising it you have already allowed the bullying to go on for too long. Without other clues to recognition, the clearest indicator that something is seriously wrong at work is likely to be your state of health. The level of stress which results is known to produce a combination of the following symptoms:

Physical	Emotional
Feeling sick	Anxiety
Sweating, shaking	Irritability
Disturbed sleep	Panic attacks
Palpitations	Depression
Loss of energy	Anger, murderous feelings
Stomach/bowl problems	Lack of motivation
Severe headaches	Loss of confidence
Loss of libido	Feeling of isolation
Minor aches and pains	Reduced self-esteem

The stress experienced by those who feel bullied often leads to strained relationships and family tension. It can also cause serious problems related to excessive use of alcohol and heavy smoking.

Chapter 9 highlights some of the difficulties that can be encountered when employees embark on a course of official confrontation, and while suggestions in this section may work in some situations but not in others, resignation is the usual response where the bully has ultimate power, and where personnel departments do not exist. In many instances, the most usual response to bullying is to resign – either as a last resort, or because health has been adversely affected.

There is little choice for employees in businesses run by a bullying boss, or schools where the bullying head is in an overall position of power. When schoolteachers and lecturers are faced with this particular situation, they must usually rely on a bullying head for the reference they require. Given the circumstances, it is unlikely that this will be an accurate reflection of the person's true qualities. The content may even sabotage any attempt to leave and find a new job. Teachers may find it helpful to seek more realistic references from senior colleagues or governors. The obvious differences between these references and those supplied by the bully should be picked up by any prospective employer. Questions arising ought to provide an opportunity for the teacher to present their side of the story. Copies of all references should be retained. Maintain continuous union contact.

Avoidance techniques

Before applying for a new job, find out if the school or company concerned is already known to your union, and if so, why?

Keep an eye on advertisements for new posts. If the same one continues to reappear as the weeks pass, it may be that the organisation concerned has a difficult headteacher or managing director. Some careful background research through your union or other sources might prove invaluable before applying.

If you are already being bullied, or about to embark on that course of official confrontation, it is vital to conserve your emotional strength and look at options for coping with this type of stress.

A 10-point survival plan

1. If counselling is available at work, make an appointment to talk through your experience.
2. If counselling is not offered by your organisation, find out if any counselling service is available in your area.
3. Tell your doctor what is happening to you at work.
4. Make a conscious effort to eat a balanced diet to try to keep well.
5. Avoid taking tranquillisers or antidepressants. They

may make you feel less able to maintain a good performance at work, just at a time when mistakes will attract the bully's unwanted attention.

6. Learn how to relax. If no relaxation classes are offered locally, cassettes are available for home use. Your nearest library should be able to help.

7. Try to keep your sense of humour.

8. Maintain contact with friends outside work. You will need good listeners.

9. However deflated you might be feeling, make time to do the things you enjoy doing outside office hours. Give yourself treats.

10. Consider assertiveness training if it is not being offered by your organisation. It will help you to cope more effectively in the future.

PART TWO

The Causes

You can kill a person only once,
but when you humiliate him,
you kill him many times over.
The Talmud

6
The Psychology of the Bully

If there is anything that we wish to change in the child, we should first examine it and see whether it is not something that could be better changed in ourselves.
Carl Gustav Jung, 'On the Development of Personality'

It was Freud who first traced the way in which a child can take on the characteristics of an adult who is aggressive towards them. He explored the process by which a child identifies with an aggressor – who is often, but not necessarily, a parent – and takes inside themselves the behaviour and attitudes to which they themselves are subjected. In their turn, the child displays this behaviour in subsequent relationships. Freud describes this process as identification with the aggressor.

In his mammoth study *The Anatomy of Human Destructiveness*, Erich Fromm gives a superb description of this identification process:

The child's tantrums, his crying, his stubbornness, the different ways in which he tries to battle with adults, are among the most visible manifestations of his attempt to have an effect, to move, to change, to express his will. The child is usually defeated by the superior strength of the adult, but the defeat does not remain without consequences; it would seem to activate a tendency to overcome the defeat by doing actively what one was forced to endure passively: in short, to do what one was forced to suffer, or to do what one was forbidden to do.

Stephen, a former NCO (Non-Commissioned Officer) in the army, describes this identification process. In his family, physical bullying was ever present:

'Dad was in the army and away a lot, so Mother was the governor when he wasn't around. Sometimes she would just shout at me and tell me to "bloody shut up or you'll get a backhander". It was usually a slap across the face. When Dad came home, and we were cheeky or came in late, we'd get a belt across the backs of the legs. My older sisters constantly bullied me, especially the eldest, who was ten at the time. She used to hurl me across the room. When my younger sister was six, I did the same to her, pulling her hair or taking her sweets. I was a bully at school, too. When I joined the army, I was often kicked and punched, and on one occasion, when I was found on the wrong accommodation block, the sergeant shoved his paystick up my nose and lifted me off the ground until my nostril split. At twenty-eight I was court-martialled for bullying a young soldier. I'd urinated on his boot during a training exercise.'

This example illustrates the chain reaction of abuse. As Fromm described, once children such as Stephen and his sisters are rendered powerless to defend themselves against their parents' physical aggression, they can be left with an unconscious feeling of being both frightened and furious. But what can they do with their fury? Where can it go? Stephen's account of family life shows the difference between anger that is expressed to which you can respond, and anger which you are left with as the result of an earlier experience. It is this feeling of being dumped on which can be so dangerous.

Mother hits son. Son is left feeling furious. Son hits sister, and so on. It is the beginning of a cycle of violence which starts within the family and moves out. From this it is clear why bullies need to be seen to be strong. It is as if they are saying 'Never again will I be weak. Never again will I be seen to be vulnerable. I am going to give someone else the experience of being defeated, and feeling humiliated.' Anger is literally passed around.

Appropriate and inappropriate anger

Erich Fromm differentiates between 'aggression with the aim to damage and the self-assertive aggression that only facilitates the pursuit of a goal'. This may be intended to damage another person, or be creative, but thinking about what constitutes a beneficial or harmful outcome of the same emotion is essential. It helps us to understand the difference between the use of appropriate or inappropriate anger which lays the foundations for a child's role in the world as an adult.

For example, if a mother is appropriately angry with her child because they misbehave, she may say, 'Stop that', or 'That's enough now'. Here there is no suspension of love, just an understandable expression of anger. From this the child will learn what is or is not acceptable to their mother. They will also learn that this behaviour has an impact, and that there are consequences. The anger, however, is not intended to destroy the child; nor is the mother out of control.

The contrasting types of anger can sometimes be seen in supermarkets. Like all situations, a shopping trip might be regarded by a young child as an opportunity to play. Problems crop up when children start to remove items from the shelves. The parent's response is crucial in both the following examples.

In the first, the mother gently removes a large packet of sweets from her son's hand and, having put it back on the shelf, leads him away. Firmly but lovingly, she explains why he should not touch. Without fuss he takes her hand as she continues.

Another mother, seeing her daughter pulling out packets of sweets, blows her top, hits the child and screams, 'How many times have I told you not to touch? You just don't know how to behave . . .' The child is devastated and begins crying inconsolably as the furious mother drags her along. Her fury, however, is out of all proportion to the incident.

In the first example, the use of appropriate anger through firm and loving management achieved the same effect as the second approach in stopping the unwanted behaviour. But in her efforts to produce the same result, the second mother got out of control. It is from this inappropriate anger that the child will suffer, and be left to deal with its legacy in later life.

The abused bully

In his major study on child abuse, *Soul Murder*, Leonard Shengold, a New York psychoanalyst, explores the consequences of 'household totalitarianism'. When a parent abuses the love of a child, he argues, the child's faith in the idea of a benevolent world is eroded by its betrayal. Through the concept of repetition-compulsion, he explores the way in which victims of such childhood encounters have an urge to repeat the experience of being abused. Those who continue into adult life as tormentors will need to go over and over the same ground, to seek situations where they can replicate the experience of tormenting. They are not necessarily concerned with understanding this repeating pattern, but are seeking to deal with it by living it out.

To some bullies, the idea of a stable environment – either at work, or in ordinary human relations – would be untenable. At one level they can function or feel secure only in an unstable environment which resembles the 'totalitarian household'. People with whom they work can be drawn into this unhealthy environment and unwittingly be forced to play a role in it.

Sadism and the bully

In attempting to understand why someone who has been abused might become either a tormentor themselves, or a victim, it is essential to realise that the two can be closely linked.

One permutation centres around masochism. An individual may not be satisfied unless they repeat the pattern of being hurt again and again. In fact this expectation needs to be constantly met. While at one level it is not what they really want, at another it brings satisfaction because they may unconsciously think: I deserve to be treated badly.

A second permutation involves the individual's sadistic trait. Some children who are brought up by at least one doting parent can develop a very narcissistic part of themselves. Their mother may have communicated to them that whatever wrong they did, in her eyes they were still wonderful. The parents of convicted murderers are often adamant, for example, that 'their boy' is innocent, convinced that he could not possibly have committed any crime.

Such individuals do not grow out of this childhood feeling that they are the centre of the universe and can do no wrong. They believe that the world must see them as they see themselves. Their fury is evident in their capacity to persecute people who do not meet these needs. In their view, other people are the cause of their problems, yet they do not really want to take responsibility for other people's feelings as a result of their actions. Such egocentric individuals loathe people who do not fall in with their idea of themselves, although they are contemptuous of those who do. They see themselves as 'golden', and feel that they can get away with anything, because whatever happens, they will triumph in the end. Their unconscious aim is to control others and make them subservient.

That said, many bullies use aggression as a form of self-defence. They report how important it is to keep others at a safe distance so that no one gets the better of them. It is my own belief, however, that this distancing is also related to a fear of closeness and intimacy. If they let people too near, they risk the possibility of being made to feel rejected and hurt all over again. Bullies deal with this anxiety through aggression. By finding reasons to be angry with colleagues, they keep them at bay. As children, these individuals frequently felt that loving feelings were used to manipulate them. This left them vulnerable. It is probable that certain forms of sexual harassment are linked to feelings of attraction which a person cannot handle. As with bullying, their contempt for themselves is translated into contempt for the object of their feelings.

Bullying and love

Children who felt ignored or sidelined by a parent figure can also develop a psychological strategy whereby aggression is an attempt to win love. The fury of being ignored is dealt with by provoking an angry response, which seems preferable to no response at all. In adult life, bullying can be a continuation of this pattern, reflecting an individual's fear that they are not lovable. Getting at work colleagues is part of the adult strategy to provoke some sort of response. However, it is ironic that by using an aggressive approach, those who most want to be loved invite rejection, fear and distrust. This, in turn, can set up a cycle of further fury which is exacerbated every time they fail in an attempt to be loved. The bully may think: If I can't win respect because of who I am, I must try to get what I want by controlling people.

I would even go so far as to say that people deprived of love in childhood may have a greater need for power, or even a greater need to be famous where ambitions are linked to gaining power, to compensate for the powerlessness they felt as a child.

Envy

In attempting to understand the psychology of the bully, it is necessary to explore its different manifestations. Where you find envy, for example, you will find the potential for bullying.

Francis, aged forty-two, is a church curate:

'Working well with children is something my vicar simply can't do, and after I introduced a family service which trebled the congregation, he became more aggressive towards me. It was the same every time I'd put a lot of work into something that was successful, like a fête or a jamboree. In the weeks following, letters from him would come through my door complaining about genuine expense claims or something I'd written in the parish magazine. The moment we were alone he would single me out and accuse me of not conforming.'

In this case, envy of another's qualities or abilities is dealt with by spoiling the potential pleasure in success, and by intimating that the individual is 'not conforming', that the problem is all theirs. This can be roughtly translated as 'I cannot deal with my envy of your abilities because it is a reminder of what is missing in me.'

In Francis's story, alleged administrative mistakes are not only used to undermine and humiliate him, they are also there as a constant reminder of who has overall power. It is, of course, entirely possible to manage others without constantly rubbing their nose in the fact that it is they who are in the subordinate role. However, it is important to distinguish between an unnecessary need to control junior colleagues, and dealing with ambitious subordinates resentful of the senior person's position. In cases such as these, a manager's anger may be a response to being attacked.

There is no doubt that many a bully is disconcerted by

the ambitions of a junior colleague, and will probably feel threatened by any real or imagined designs on their job. They may imagine, rightly or wrongly, that other people will see this person as more popular, or better organised, or more proficient at what they do. The bully's insecurity about his or her own competence will manifest itself in a desire to keep rivals down.

Anna, an English teacher, illustrates the consequence of personal envy:

> 'After I joined the teaching staff of the girls' grammar school where I'd once been an Oxford award-winner, I began to notice that the head seemed to dislike and fear anyone whom she regarded as her social and intellectual superior. She had an unconvincing genteel accent, gross table manners, and when I was speaking to someone else, she would come up and pointedly greet my colleague by name, ignoring me and anyone to whom I was speaking by shoring us apart with her shoulder. When outsiders came to staff lunches, she would introduce everyone round the table, always omitting me.'

To an outsider Anna could be regarded as over-reacting or making too much fuss, until her experience is examined closely. It is more probable that this head was giving Anna a sense of her own experience as a child. How often children report similar accounts of being humiliated or ignored! The power behind this form of bullying lies in its subtle slights that hurt the recipient but can be disguised from onlookers. The unspoken message to Anna was: 'You are not important enough to be acknowledged. You must remain on the sidelines while the important people get together.' In this there are elements of both intrusive parents, and those who exclude their children from the adult group.

However, a bully may pick up the disdain an individual

has for them. Their contempt can be a defence against the pain invoked by an earlier experience of being treated as unimportant. The aggression used to retaliate is a way of communicating that they feel hurt by your distance.

The envy of another's qualities is deeply linked to the feeling that in childhood they somehow missed out on affection and love spontaneously given. Seeing colleagues enjoying good relations at work, for example, will be a reminder to a bully that other people are able to experience a quality of life that they have never had.

At Anna's school, other difficulties revolved around the head's lack of trust:

> 'She was incapable of delegation. Important information about pupils' circumstances was not passed on to staff because we could not be trusted with anything confidential.'

Adults experience lack of delegation as being treated like a child who cannot be trusted. In understanding the behaviour of the bully, this is important evidence. The knock-on effect of a lack of trust experience in childhood is the need for control. The greater the level of being controlled or let down in earlier life, the greater the need for an adult to do everything themselves. They will delegate only inasmuch as they continue to maintain absolute control.

In general, genuine authority is derived from the respect and commitment a leader evokes – not unquestioningly, of course, but because of the trust an employee has in their integrity. This is not to say that there is no place for anger in leadership, whether it is in the home or in the workplace, but the same values apply. This type of leadership is founded on trust and genuine strength. Bullying leadership, which controls others by both threatening and carrying out threats, is based on fear. As a result of their upbringing, some managers use their power to blast people, not to manage them. They blow people up and, not surprisingly, they also make them cry.

Another element to the bully, however, is the fragile base to their seeming strength. Hand in hand with aggression comes a real fear of retaliation.

Anna completes her story:

> 'If people confronted her boldly, she collapsed. When I demanded an explanation from her after some rude, tossed-off comments, she scuttled into her personal loo and refused to emerge. But when people broke down after being insulted, she invariably dismissed their distress as ridiculous over-reaction.'

This head's response illustrates the gulf between real courage and the frightened yet frightening anger of the bully. She deprived Anna of an opportunity to respond to the impact of her actions, yet her subsequent hiding could be interpreted as running away from the consequence of her aggression. It has the feel of a little girl who hits her sister, then runs away fearing retaliation. Bullying and cowardice are closely aligned.

To those who are unaware of the chink in a bully's armour, this person will appear impenetrable. By threatening retribution if a colleague makes a complaint, the bully ensures that what is going on does not become known, and the problem is perpetuated. The power of the bully lies in frightening to such an extent that nothing is said, and people often leave organisations to survive because they feel that they are stuck in a hopeless situation. Although the power of the victim lies in the potential to speak out, who will be believed?

Jo is a twenty-eight-year-old advertising executive:

> 'When I stood up to my boss and complained, he would make the situation look silly, as if I was blowing

it up out of nothing. He always reacted in a
patronising way, speaking in a soft voice.'

As described by Gregory Bateson, and later by Ronald
Laing, the victim is made to feel as if their outrage is
irrational. The aggressor makes the victim feel as if it is
they who have a problem, which is not connected with
them in any way. Those subjected to aggression not only
feel victims of it, but are also made to doubt their own
perception of events.

Selecting victims

As we know, the school bully may single out another
pupil for a variety of reasons. At work, and in adulthood
generally, the possibilities for picking on a particular
characteristic are equally potent. They are, however,
more sophisticated than the intimidation carried out by
children and adolescents. The bully may home in on
someone who is working too slowly, or on a person who is
perceived as rather spineless. Popularity, success and
good looks are other typical targets. There are also those
who get it in the neck for having higher qualifications.
The list is endless. More important is to comprehend why
a bully selects a particular group, or goes for a specific
individual. To establish this, we need to ask certain
questions:

- Why did you single out this individual?
- What do they represent to you?
- What do you feel about them?
- What do you want to make them feel?
- Is there any part of them that you identify in yourself?

Such questions are designed to develop some thinking in
a bully to try and promote some insight into their actions.

The heartless bully

Although one image of a psychopath is that of a criminal or a particularly deranged personality, there can be psychopathic elements in some bullies which must be identified if this problem of aggression at work is to be understood.

Christine, a conciliation officer, describes a colleague:

> 'He fitted a psychopathic personality to perfection and was able to be totally detached from any conscience. He had this brilliant ability to play whatever role he wanted and be as devious as he liked, lying through his teeth to get you into trouble. If you challenged him he'd say, "I don't know why you take me so seriously. I don't mean it."'

Only an understanding of the psychopathic personality will enable us to appreciate what a tricky individual this type of bully can be.

A psychopath is defined in the *Dictionary of Psychology* as an 'individual, emotionally unstable to a degree approaching the pathological, but with no specific or marked mental disorder'. Harvey Cleckley, in his classic book *The Mask of Sanity*, considers this area so 'confused' that it is 'unparalleled' in the whole field of psychiatry. He identifies specific types of psychopathic personalities, and lists the factors he has isolated as typical: superficial and good intelligence; unreliability, untruthfulness and insincerity; lack of remorse or shame; antisocial behaviour, poor judgement and failure to learn from experience; pathological egocentricity, the incapacity to love, and a total lack of insight.

A study of the 'creative psychopath' has shown that such a person has some success in school work and interpersonal relationships, as well as some capacity for emotional involvement. The aggressive psychopath, on the other hand, is considered totally egocentric and almost beyond help. A crucial observation made by many researchers in this field is the psychopath's inability to realise the effect their actions are having on others. They do not see themselves as others do. They also believe that other people do not think differently to them.

If psychopaths do have a totally egocentric view of the world, then it is easier to understand their tendency to exhibit unreasonable behaviour, and to blame others for their own misfortunes. The central feature of the egocentric personality is that they consider that people exist for them; that their wishes should come first; that they cannot be justifiably contradicted, questioned, blamed or criticised. This self-righteousness makes them feel immune from guilt if they hurt or harm others. This irrational view of the world, if it is accepted unquestioningly by those around, would escalate their bullying behaviour. Furthermore, their total failure either to accept responsibility for their own actions, or to realise that there are various ways of viewing a situation, adversely affects the probability that they might seek help.

Not without reason does Cleckley call his book *The Mask of Sanity*. In relation to bullying, it is the failure to realise that bullies have a problem which is such an important aspect. In the example of a bully Christine related earlier, she described the well-documented ability of the psychopathic personality to charm and fool people into believing they are perfectly normal and well-balanced. However, *I want to make it clear that bullies are not psychopaths, but their make-up may consist of psychopathic elements. It is this that makes their behaviour intelligible*. The word 'bullying' can belie the degree of aggression.

Anthony Storr, who regards psychopathic behaviour as comparable to the behaviour of children and infants, questions by what mechanism a child comes to control impulsiveness and aggression. On the one hand he argues that a child who is loved by their parents will adopt the values of their parents, because to do so will invite approval and further love; to refrain from so doing will invoke the suspension of love. A child who is constantly punished and criticised for doing something wrong, however, and has had their needs and wishes constantly frustrated, cannot in adulthood tolerate any setback or frustration of their needs. In response to difficulties they become either aggressive or impulsive. It is this compulsion to have one's needs met at all costs that is such an important feature of the bully.

Unhealthy alliances

Bullies can achieve greater power from the selective associations they make. The study of organisations reveals that they create many unofficial roles for colleagues, including henchmen, spies, lackeys, sycophants or court jester. To be in favour with an aggressor might seem like the best way to survive. The protection it offers might seem to free you from fear, although the bully who has favourites creates terrible rivalries in the working group. Those who are out of favour deeply resent those they feel receive special treatment; this can lead to a working environment with an in and an out group, fostering secretive behaviour, clans, cliques and clandestine operations. The favoured members feel at times untouchable; the others feel pushed out. The risk to the favoured is that they can lose their status by falling out of favour. This culture is divisive, destructive and ultimately brings out the worst elements in individuals.

Carolyn, a charity worker, recalls her experience of one such boss:

'She surrounded herself with people who wouldn't contradict her. Outside the office, she was always inviting them to dinner, or buying them presents and doing favours. On one occasion, soon after I took up my new job, I noticed that everyone else was meekly agreeing with things she was saying about a mutual colleague. I disagreed because I knew them to be untrue, and after that she completely ignored me. I suppose she must have realised that here was a person who would never be in her power.'

The bully in this example underpins her control by establishing a group of 'yes' men and women. If you do not fit into the role ascribed to you, you risk being kept out – literally not invited to the party. Consequently, in some organisations, it is those with integrity who become the victims of bullies. It is the failure to control you that exacerbates their inner fury.

The bully can confuse consensus with correctness. Just because everyone agrees with them, it does not mean they are right. However, some bullies will not accept any criticism or allow disagreement. They protect themselves from criticism in their choice of close colleagues.

Sheila, aged thirty, is a secretary:

'He builds up a wall around himself by cultivating certain people who cannot see what he is really like, or, in most cases, know very well but choose to support him to avoid trouble.'

Members of the organisation can be treated like cohorts. They are expected to agree loyally and not question the master. Some bullies, however, have a secret contempt for those who just go along with them, but they also have a secret fear of those who disagree.

What can be deduced from the two examples above is the fragility of organisations based on fear-engendered alliances. This quality of alliance is very different from strong relationships made at work which contribute to a strong team.

Gangs

It is not only individuals who bully at work. Groups of individuals bully others, too; just as gangs are formed in adolescence, so too can they operate in the workplace. Ganging up against an individual can take many forms.

Lisa, aged twenty-eight, is a nurse:

> 'When I was working in a mental hospital in Wales, I complained to senior staff after I saw the nursing auxiliaries using the same unchanged bowl of water to wash dozens of incontinent patients. After further complaints, I was "sent to Coventry" for the whole of each seven-hour shift. I was also ignored by my senior colleagues and locked out of the office during tea breaks. When it was time to go home, I'd find my tyres let down. Letters used to arrive in my pigeonhole saying: "You're going to regret what you've done". My days were full of verbal nastiness and cloaked threats.'

'Sending someone to Coventry' continues to take place, as does excluding individuals and intimidating others, not necessarily just one person. A gang may be formed within a layer of a company, or between layers. Some of these groups are described as 'the heavy mob' or 'the mafia'. This idea of the pack, of marauding groups, might appear alien, but it is the adult equivalent of the adolescent gang that everyone feared and steered clear of. It may be held together by a strong 'leader', or by a common interest, or perhaps by similar backgrounds.

Gangs in the form of a team can bully upwards – for example, by sabotaging the directives of their manager, or by making them feel useless. Gossip can be a by-product of bullying: deliberately spreading stories that could hurt or harm someone's reputation, perhaps hoping it will get back to them. Malicious gossip comes under the umbrella of bullying, in that it may be a cowardly way of hurting someone without the target knowing what the source of the rumour is. Some unions have also abused their power in the past, and active members have been described as bullyboys, using dubious tactics to manipulate the workforce.

In some organisations, very senior managers and directors are employed as 'hatchet men' and given authority to do whatever is necessary to get a company on its feet. They wield enormous power, which they use ruthlessly. They may have been chosen for this reason, and perhaps their own background has predisposed them to be able to shed blood without losing sleep. On the other hand, they may simply feel that their own job will be safe only if they carry out the unpleasant tasks required of them at all costs.

As Alan, a managing director, observed:

> 'If an organisation has spent a lot of money bringing that person in, he or she won't quite have *carte blanche*, but in the first few months they will have a hell of a lot of freedom in which to impose their character . . . whatever the consequences.'

Every day on the roads, drivers try to bully others in a variety of ways: by coming up behind, for example, and trying to make the person in front go faster; or controlling them, perhaps, by going slowly. Central to this whole area is the wish to force people to do what they want them to do. Like the reckless driver who doesn't give way, the bully tries to force his or her targets to bend to their will. How you, as an individual, respond to this provocation is critical. If you work with a bully, then it can be akin to being with a disturbed adolescent, with all the attendant disruption and anxiety. In dealing with the bully, as with other adolescents, the same principles apply. The adult, however, is potentially more destructive. As Donald Winnicott wisely observed: 'no adults are all the time adult. This is because people are not just their own age; they are to some extent every age and no age.'

Neil Crawford
1992

7
The Bullies

'If I saw someone free from hang-ups being happy it really got up my nose. I'd think: You've got it easy, you haven't suffered like I have yet'

After David, aged thirty-five, was unexpectedly promoted to the position of head chef in a West Country hotel, his bullying was at its worst. As the product of a violent childhood and the experiences of previous bosses who terrorised their kitchen staff, David could not accept anything less than perfection in his professional role:

'At twenty-four I was suddenly made up to acting head chef just after I'd started a new job, and although I knew the theory, I'd never had to put it into practice, so it was a lot of responsibility. Deep down, I suppose, I was unsure whether I could do the job. I was in charge of the kitchen, the menus, official functions, the restaurant, stock control, kitchen porters and five other chefs, but no one had told me about "man management". When I came under pressure, I did bully the staff, but standards were sloppy when I took over, so I decided to assert my authority – not only to get the job done, but to gain respect. As far as I was concerned, they were going to have to learn the hard way like I had. The kitchens I had already worked in were ruled with fear, with cruelty even. In one restaurant, in Switzerland, the chefs would get out the knives and we'd be chased round the kitchen. One apprentice was beaten up because he messed up the soup. There was no talking, and we worked with heads bowed in an atmosphere of verbal violence, but we certainly learnt to produce a high standard of cuisine.

'Once I was in charge of my own kitchen, if I saw an apprentice getting cocky, I'd decide to take him down a peg or two by criticising everything he did, all the time finding fault and looking for improvement. I would scream, and bawl and swear at them, and tear them to pieces in front of the others. If I didn't like their presentation I'd pick up their work and chuck it on the floor. I didn't trust other people to get it right, and because I felt under such tremendous personal pressure, I would never take days off, so then I got tired and niggly. One morning, as I arrived at the hotel, an apprentice charged out of the door and shouted at me to fuck off. Inside, tables had been overturned, plates smashed, there were eggs and flour all over the kitchen walls. He'd just flipped, but I knew there had been days when I'd set out to make his life a misery. He had the potential to be a good chef, but he got on my nerves because he didn't have the right attitude towards self-discipline so that I constantly criticised everything he did. I can remember thinking: Why don't they get it into their heads that there's a job to be done? They shouldn't be able to laugh a lot. Although I wished I could be like that, if I saw someone who was free from hang-ups being happy it really got up my nose. I'd think: You've got it easy, you haven't suffered like I have yet, you don't know what life is about. I was feeling strong in one way, because even after all I'd been through, I had survived.

'It certainly never occurred to me that I bullied anyone, although I did notice that one chef was so knocked flat after I'd had a go at him that I couldn't get any work out of him for the rest of the day. I'd see him shaking all right, but I didn't realise it would destroy him. Another chef, who was very talented, was also rather a weak person, so even when I piled on the work he'd just take it and say, "Yes, chef". That's all he ever said – "Yes, chef". I put him under pressure because I knew he was reliable. I also knew I could get away with it, but that really annoyed me because he had no nerve, no get-up-and-go. I saw him as a wimp, I suppose, but one day he turned round and punched me, and that made me think. I wondered what I had done to make him do that. Had I been making his life a misery? But it didn't make any difference. I kept piling on the stuff, and eventually he left. But you have to take the mickey out of people. Teasing them and sending them up is a matter of survival, because other people do it to you. It's part of the cut and thrust of going to work. If I can make a remark that puts someone down, it makes me feel powerful.

I've always disliked authority because of my violent upbringing, but I grew up wanting to be in authority, wanting to be in control of my own life.

'As an only child I remember my dad wanting to completely dominate me and my mother. His father was the same. He terrorised my grandmother, and ruled all five kids with fear, yet in the local town people thought he was a nice bloke. It was the same with my dad. All my schoolfriends thought he was great, and everyone in the surrounding villages who knew him would say, "What a lovely man". At the school where he worked they thought the world of him, and certainly outside the home he was a very popular person. In the home there was a complete lack of love. He was constantly shouting at me, and if I wanted to force any encouragement out of him, whatever I did had to be excellent. Then, if I was lucky, I might get the odd mumble. He acted as if he wasn't interested, although I suspect he probably was. We had a big garden, and when Dad asked me to go and help him, there was no father-and-son-having-a-good-time sort of relationship. If I didn't pull up a weed, or if I accidentally trod on a plant, he would whack me across the head every time.

'I remember one particular incident, when I was about ten, which was particularly distressing. I was watching TV when he sent me to my room because I hadn't written any birthday thank-you letters to my aunts and uncles. So I went upstairs, put a record on, and set about doing them at once. Within a few minutes he came storming in, fuming that I couldn't possibly do two things at once, took off the record and smashed it on the floor. Then he started chasing me round the bed, shouting, "You little bugger, you little sod, you do as you're told." He went berserk, and I can remember thinking: I was doing what he asked, why doesn't he leave me alone? When I was older, he'd complain if I switched on the TV and say, "Who do you think pays the licence?" At other times I'd say, "Dad, can I put the TV on?" and he'd say, "You don't have to ask me, son, this is your home," so you just couldn't win. He was a trade-union shop steward at one time, and it was almost as if he thrived on arguments so that he could prove his intellectual prowess. 'When I was sixteen, after going to church every Sunday throughout my childhood, he told me one day that my parents weren't going to force me to go any more if I'd rather not, that I was old enough to make my own choices. The moment I said, "Okay, I don't want to come to church", he just picked me up, pinned me against the wall and started banging my head. Then, with his face pushed right up against mine, he went into the most vile temper I've ever seen and said, "Right, then you're going to join the army, I'm putting you in the army." I left home before he had a chance. I once challenged him, and called him an out-and-out bully for always ripping me to pieces, but he just argued. My mother is a very sweet, calm, wise woman who never loses her temper, but I'm only just talking to her about these things now. Neither of them can figure out why I eventually had a nervous breakdown.

'As a schoolboy I was an absolute bag of nerves, my headmaster was feared by the four hundred pupils and all the staff. Whenever any of us complained about his tyrannical behaviour to our parents, it was all put down to the difficult job of running a school, and we weren't believed.

'Later in life, as a chef, I used alcohol as a way of relieving my fear, because when I was sober I couldn't cope. When I was working at the West Country hotel, a new manager constantly criticised me and did everything to put me down and try to undermine my knowledge. It made me feel like giving him a good thumping. I can see now that my own bullying behaviour has affected every area of my life, including friendships. Recently, a woman colleague who had been quite friendly suddenly turned haughty and refused to speak to me. I actually felt her hatred and I thought: What have I done here? When I eventually asked her, she told me I was patronising and condescending and treated her as if she didn't have a brain in her head; that I was always barging into her territory, always telling her what to do, always trying to take control. I apologised and thanked her for telling me, but I don't think that at the time it really sank in. Using sarcasm instead of your fists is just as damaging, especially if deep down you are feeling inferior.'

David wrote to the BBC after hearing another bully discuss his experience in 'Whose Fault Is It Anyway?'. It was, he said, like listening to himself on the radio, and it made his flesh creep. He has since turned to his belief in God to help him change, and now that he can recognise his own behaviour, he finds he is able to avoid working out his own fear and resentment on others.

'I had a basic distrust of others, and found it very difficult to delegate. I had this sense of intellectual superiority that I knew how to do a job better than anyone else.'

Brian is a forty-six-year-old civil servant who now recognises the destructiveness of his own behaviour. He grew up in a permanent state of anxiety in an all-female household dominated by his tyrannical grandmother. He has sought to retain control of his own life ever since. When Brian was eleven, his grandmother died. He remembers whistling for joy at her funeral.

'One Sunday afternoon, as a small child, I was given a toy which I accidentally broke almost immediately. I can remember my grandmother shouting at me in such a way that it made me feel totally inadequate. Afterwards, I withdrew into a spare bedroom and just stood, in the middle, noticing other broken toys. I had no idea if I had been responsible, but either way, it reinforced a feeling of being destroyed by this attitude towards me from a person I detested. As a child I was never praised or encouraged, just criticised, and to make sure people didn't treat me like that again, as I grew up I fought back.

'I inflicted the pain I carried from my past on to others, mostly through little comments that would undermine them and keep them at a safe distance. I became skilled at putting in a pre-emptive strike before I came under attack and faced the possibility of being destroyed all over again. I developed a persona which intimidated people, and I was really good at it.

'At school everyone steered clear of me. No one bullied me. At work I perceived everyone as a threat, but I was good at arguing, and if you can debate well, it keeps other people under your control. It also conceals your own feelings of inadequacy. I had a basic distrust of others, and found it very difficult to delegate. I had this sense of intellectual superiority that I knew how to do a job better than anyone else. I wasn't willing to listen to what anyone else had to say, and if they wanted to do anything in opposition, I would put up every barrier. They would be well aware of the consequences if they tried to get something through off their own bat. I'd always analyse the individual's personality and identify the weak points to home in on later if the going got rough; if they should in any way pose some sort of threat. If I could see that someone lacked confidence, for example, and that person wasn't too proficient with computers, I'd put them in charge of that section, knowing they couldn't cope. In a subtle and manipulative way I'd go out to destroy them, to disarm. Keeping people at a distance was a way of surviving. It made me feel safe. It put me in control, so that no one would bully me.

'I never recognised myself as a bully. I would have described myself as abrasive – not only to people beneath me, but also to those above. I was impatient, I'd make sharp, cutting remarks, and I never gave people the space to do things themselves. I'd hover around and keep checking everything they did. It made me feel in control, even though I probably wasn't. If I felt myself getting out of control, especially under pressure, it built up into a tremendous tension, and that's when I took it out on other people.

'At one time in my career I had a manager whose way of motivating people was to jump up and down and shout at them. He'd come into your room, and it didn't matter if the door was open so that everyone else could hear. I started to learn from that behaviour. In many ways it seemed that the organisation found it acceptable. It certainly appeared to guarantee success because there were many other managers acting in similar ways, and getting promotion in spite of it, so what message would you get from that? If you're working in an authoritarian environment which takes the view that its employees are a lazy lot of sods who need a kick up the backside from time to time, then no one is going to challenge your bullying behaviour, and you're not going to change.

'I've never been a relaxed type of person, so my bullying wasn't confined to my working life. I was aggressive and intimidating at home, too, and if my wife ever confronted me, I'd simply outdebate her. My mother was so bullied by my grandmother that it affected the way I looked at other women. To me they appeared inferior, requiring to be dominated. Even now my mother is terrible at communicating, and although I'm learning to articulate my feelings, I know that for a long time people at work have found it difficult to communicate with me. As far as I was concerned, communication meant exposing my own vulnerabilities, and to do that would mean loss of control. The way to survive was to cut people off altogether. When my grandmother died I was shocked that I had no recollection of her looking after me, because I'd blocked most of it out. I do remember sensing constant tension between the two most important people in my life – my mother and my grandmother – and it has left me feeling envious, not only of those who have had it easier, but of those who have benefited from the kind of childhood I never had.'

How Brian has been helped:

'It's only when you start to become aware of different models of behaviour that you can begin the very difficult business of undoing the learning processes that have been with you for a long time. For me it happened when I went on training courses on how to deal effectively with people. Group therapy helped, too, by getting me to understand the way in which my experiences in childhood affected my responses to other adult relationships. I also changed jobs and joined an organisation which promotes a conciliatory attitude towards others. Here there are almost no rumours – about jobs being changed, or mergers or financial crises. Everything is communicated at all levels, so everyone knows what is happening on a day-to-day basis and therefore feels more secure. If I find myself reverting back to my old ways, I can cut it out quite quickly, but I rely on my wife to sharpen my perception of myself, and of my behaviour towards others. Becoming better at communication has helped me not only to trust others, but also to be more honest and open about my own vulnerabilities. I suppose the real turning point came when I noticed that my eldest child, aged six, was using the same manipulative behaviour towards me as I had used towards everybody else. I was shocked. This was history repeating itself.'

8
The Psychology
of the Bullied

'It is possible not to be responsible for a problem yet still to be responsible for its solutions.'
Linda Sandford, *Strong at the Broken Places*

The effects of bullying on individuals, families and even whole groups have been powerfully described in the first part of this book. Fear, self-doubt, impotence, rage, all surface in these disturbing accounts, though perhaps the most pervasive impression is that of the victim's bewilderment, and sense of shock, that this could even be happening to them at all.

Some people are bullied, and the problem resides solely with the bully. It has no justification and just makes their working life intolerable. However, in order to understand why one person and not another is being bullied, it is important to consider how residues from one's past may be operating in the present.

Looking at the legacy that individuals inherit from their earlier family life is the clue to understanding both the bully and the bullied. Some bullies have the knack of picking up the weaknesses of those close to them, including colleagues at work. It has frequently been my experience that a difficult relationship at work can be understood only if it is looked at as a re-creation of earlier relationships. Obviously it will not be the same, but it may contain similar ingredients.

Liz, a training executive, found herself in this situation:

'I kept on wondering: Why me? Why does he pick on me while he is so charming to others? I couldn't understand why I felt so defeated by what was happening when I'd always managed to pull myself out of other situations at work. It was only through counselling that I discovered he had tapped into things from my past about not feeling good enough. He had triggered all my old childhood patterns of being bullied by my mother. She is an unpleasant little woman who was very very violent and aggressive and who constantly criticised me and my two brothers. She is also quite charming, very articulate and intelligent. I would never have made a connection between her and the man who was bullying me at work.'

It is not uncommon, however, to encounter traits of one parent in a work colleague of the opposite sex, as well as the same sex. An individual can have had no previous problems of a bullying nature until they come across a colleague who stirs up feelings associated with figures from their earlier life. When this happens, the impact can be such that it arouses similar responses.

Bill, the schoolteacher who told his story in Chapter 5, describes a situation not unlike that experienced by Liz, but with a more concrete link between past and present:

'A thought sprang into my mind one evening while I was doing the washing-up and it made a twisted, awful sense. I realised the bully physically resembled my mother in crucial ways; she even narrowed her eyes at me when she was angry. As an only child I had a mother who doted on me, who would have breathed for me if she could, but she was also intensely bossy and I was terrified of her. I remember as a child daubing charcoal all over my face, as makeshift war paint for a game of cowboys andIndians. Later, when I was rushing to be home by five o'clock, I was halfway there when I realised I hadn't removed the charcoal. I dashed back to my friend's house to scrub it off because I was terrified of the consequences – not of being late, but of being found in a dirty state, because my mother was so obsessed with cleanliness.'

At first sight, Bill's description of his mother as doting suggests a loving person. But does the idea of a loving relationship rest easily with his description of being terrified? What Bill seems to describe is a dominant, overbearing and obsessional character, resembling the bully in his working life. Living with the fear of being reprimanded can evoke enormous dread. It can carry on into adult life as a conscious or unconscious anxiety that you will be disapproved of or attacked by people in authority. In Bill's family the experience of an environment in which you could be punished if you 'got it wrong' will have left a legacy that would affect his entire adult life.

Adapting to a parental environment which is punishing can involve developing a placatory disposition where protecting oneself from attack or disapproval becomes a central motivation. However, some very complicated processes can be set in motion. Dependence on the mother, and the wish for her approval, can result in the child's unwillingness to express their anger directly. Although as an adult it can be easy to forget how devastating it is for a child to experience the temporary withdrawal of love, the anger and hurt are still held within the child. And as we will explore, when anger goes underground, it is often expressed in covert ways.

When children are brought up in a disturbed family, they often feel victims of their parents' own problems. And as parents are the model for their own children's behaviour, patterns of response are passed on from generation to generation. And this cycle can be broken only when one generation gains insight into this psychological inheritance.

Edward, a civil servant aged forty-four, has attempted to explore his past with the objective of discovering its impact on his life.

'As I was growing up, my father's needs always came first. On the surface he seemed jovial and playful, but this amusing front masked his aggression, which would always come out if we went too far. Although to an outsider everything would appear fairly normal, aggression was always just below the surface. I was always getting into trouble for feeding the dog, and if my mother caught me dropping a piece of meat to him, she would shout at me. I identified with this animal, whom I loved, because I felt he was like me. I, too, spent my life hanging around hoping I would be noticed.

'Everything had to be done in a certain way and my mother would hover over me, making sure the knives were dried properly. I remember being hit round the face by her and always being accused of stealing biscuits. Part of my growing up was always being scolded; getting it wrong and feeling invaded. My sister, whom I bullied, was the butt of my aggression. I loved her, but whom else could I hurt? She teased me and provoked me, but she must have felt very angry with me. My father, I think, found it difficult to tolerate the fact that I had opportunities as a child that he didn't, and while he professed an interest in me and encouraged my development, he envied me. There was never any sign that he might understand how I could be feeling if I expressed concern. In fact my memory is one of parents who communicated fear in their attempts to hide from the experience of my growing up. They didn't naturally relate to children, and life was a series of shoulds and should nots. To ask for anything would be to risk rejection and be told I was greedy.

'Later in life I felt frightened to ask for things which

it would be appropriate to expect. I developed a need to do everything myself so that I wouldn't have to ask for anything and risk further rejection. Secretly, I felt that people should be available to fulfill my needs, which should come first. It was the opposite, I suppose, of what had happened where it was always me who had to wait. It's as if my childhood was a failed attempt by my parents to control me by making me into the person they wanted me to be. My development was so skewed that it left me with enough psychological baggage to last a lifetime. I have had to be helped to understand how all these things that happened at home affected relationships in my adult life.'

Many people feel victims for not having had the start in life they might have hoped for. They feel handicapped by the absence of opportunities for development and of an environment in which they feel they could have flourished. Some individuals do well despite troubled circumstances. However, whatever the degree of difficulties within family life, a 'victim' will remain in this role unless they begin to work on and understand how their character and relationships are operating on a daily basis. Each day, when they are at work, their history is unconsciously influencing their present relationships.

Psychological aggression

If we are to understand both the bully and the victim, it is important to look at the concept of psychological aggression. This is an umbrella term which refers to behaviour which inhibits development in a child, and is aggressive in that it can be hurtful and humiliating. It is not present only in the obvious angry outburst, but in many subtle forms which leave the recipient feeling bad.

In family life, for example, it can be observed in the following scenarios:

- The father who clearly prefers one child over another.
- The mother who prematurely expects her child to be an adult.
- Parents who do not want to give up anything for their children.
- Parents' unavailability and unwillingness to understand a child's fears.
- A parent's inability to see their son or daughter as a separate person.

This type of aggression is present in a variety of forms at work as well – for example, in a colleague who refuses to make time to meet so that you can never sort out a problem. When you speak in a meeting, you are made to feel that your contribution is not worthwhile because no one takes up what you say. If appreciation is not offered but must always be sought, this, too, is a form of aggression.

Psychological consequences

If a victim's feelings are neither expressed nor explored, being bullied can leave them feeling both furious and frightened. If an aggressor has established control through fear, the frightened one, not daring to speak, is left with the conflict. If they confront the aggressor, or blow the whistle and make a complaint, they fear recriminations or whatever consequences may have been threatened. If they say nothing at all, they are left with their angry and frightened feelings. Typical manifestations of this conflict are lethargy, paralysis and a sense of hopelessness.

Depression is one consequence of keeping fury under control. Keeping anger buried is a way of dealing with it by literally deadening it, but the psychological price may be high. Controlling anger is exhausting to cope with, and the knock-on effect requires considerable emotional energy. Enthusiasm is inhibited as a result, and this in turn affects the capacity to work. The result can be psychological impotence, which is often managed by turning aggression in on oneself. Suicidal feelings are the most extreme form of self-hatred, although there are many others. For example, an individual may come to regard themselves as being of no worth where an aggressor has persistently found fault. This manifests itself in a sense of emptiness and lack of confidence, even an expectation that they deserve to be treated badly.

Given their deep-rooted anger and feelings of impotence as bullied adults, it is hardly surprising that these men and women find their lives dominated by what is taking place at work. Their need to talk about the experience with sympathetic people is very great. In a sense, they need to relieve themselves of the intolerable nature of the stress, although this is likely to have repercussions. By passing on the fury and the hurt to those closest to them, these people can also become victims of the same conflict, albeit one step removed. I am always struck by the amount of time, both in and out of work, that is taken up by discussing bullying and aggression.

Appeasement of a bully

In adulthood it is common for people to try to pacify an aggressor rather than tackle them. The wish to placate can stem from a deep-rooted need to be loved, and a misguided belief that if one appeases an aggressor they will cease their attack. In fact, this response increases the likelihood of attack. As long as a bully feels that they can 'get away with it', they will continue. The psychological profile of a victim must therefore include an unwillingness to confront a tormentor with the effect they are having on others. This amounts to collusion with the aggressor.

Impotent anger and revenge

Associated with being a victim of aggression may be feelings of worthlessness. The victim takes into themselves the role ascribed to them; but often, hidden away, are feelings of revenge. A part of them is saying: 'They're not going to get away with it. Some day they will pay.'

In many cases a fine line divides being a bully and being a victim. In either case, this wish for revenge may surface in adult life. When an individual literally feels filled with anger, the buried injustices they carry from another period of their life may erupt into the present. When they feel in a stronger position, they will exact revenge on people over whom they now have power.

Working with a person like this can leave you with few options: to do his bidding and feel resentful about being controlled; to fight and risk perpetual conflict; or to find a way of protecting yourself. Each of these requires thought, and it is this which can dominate your life to the exclusion of your work and, potentially, your peace of mind. The feeling of impotence and anger that bullying engenders can get out of control.

Ron, a designer, recalls the violent fantasies he had about his boss, who bullied him relentlessly over a period of six years:

> 'I often had very unchristian thoughts about beating him up, and at one stage, if someone had given me a loaded revolver, I would have put it to his head. I tried not to let hatred come into it, but I just wanted him to stop. On the way to a union meeting one night I was shouting in the car, "Why doesn't he stop it, why, why?" That's when I knew I had to get control of myself.'

What is striking – and common – about Ron's fantasies is that they were so powerful, and so pervasive, that he was

103

finally frightened by them himself. This example highlights the victim's feeling of being driven mad, and the
wish for a release from the incomprehension and despair
they are experiencing. The fantasies reflect their feeling of
powerlessness. In reality they feel impotent. Only in their
imagination can the situation be resolved. The vicelike
grip in which a bully can hold their victims should never
be underestimated. Nor should one underestimate the
potency of the bullied. It is not uncommon for them to
feel murderous, or to hope that an accident will befall the
aggressor, and become preoccupied with feelings of
revenge.

The other victims

Working in an organisation with a bully will eventually
require a decision about how to handle what is happening.

In many cases both those who stand up for themselves
and those who are unable to are on the receiving end of
aggression. Someone who leaves a company, or transfers,
might appear less of a victim than someone who remains
in the same environment. By getting out, they argue: 'I
am not going to tolerate this any more, I am not going to
be in a position where I allow another to disrupt my life
and victimise me.' Many people would view freedom from
a tyrant as more important than the loss of a job, and
consider that holding on to one's psychological well-being
represents an unwillingness to be a victim. Others, however, would argue that their decision to leave represents a
triumph for tyranny, for they show themselves to be
victims by being forced out at a time not of their own
choosing. After all, where do they go? To a better job, or
simply into unemployment?

An aggressor may well experience their departure as a
triumph, while the person who leaves may bear both a
sense of failure and a reinforced identity as a victim. The
person who stays despite life at work being hell, who will

104

not be forced to lose what is rightfully theirs, may be perceived as the stronger. It can be argued both ways. Nevertheless, leaving an organisation does, at the very least, deprive an aggressor of further opportunity to bully, and saves the victim from more hurt.

It is sometimes surprising what reactions handing in one's notice can evoke. Jack had his life made as difficult as possible by his primary-school head, who constantly undervalued his work and refused to implement a co-ordinating role that he had been given by the previous head, which would have given him greater status in the school. He was the only male member of staff, and she would refer to the whole staff group as 'ladies'.

After months of feeling defeated, Jack applied for another job and was successful. He had not burnt his bridges by resigning in advance, and when he did eventually hand in his notice, his head became very distressed, telling him how she was struggling in the job. Before his very eyes she became a pathetic creature. By contrast, his decision to leave, but in his own time, had restored his self-respect. He now felt liberated, even strong. Jack also found himself in a very common predicament: by being sympathetic and ministering to this woman, he was the victim comforting the aggressor.

The victim as aggressor

If an element in some bullies is a sadistic pleasure in hurting others, or the need to release aggression through intimidation, are there types of people who are more willing recipients?

An alleged victim of bullying may actually provoke anger in others, yet be totally unconscious of their part in the process. They may unwittingly set up a situation which re-creates an earlier relationship. At one level it is a model with which they are already familiar. People who talk too much, for example, and seem uninterested in

105

anyone else, can be infuriating. What is their constant chattering really about? It can, in fact, be a way of literally getting something out of people, perhaps to bolster their own self-esteem through the attention sought, but it can leave the person at whom it is directed feeling drained, flat, angry or bored. If the recipient of this chatter feels they have little to give, they may respond by exploding, rejecting the individual, or overtly expressing their anger. In turn, the chatterer may describe themselves as being bullied.

The failure to make the connection between the aggression they are communicating through their chatter, and the response it engenders in others, exemplifies how tricky the whole business can become. The victim as aggressor can also be the silent member of the organisation. If they do not share their feelings, and make no contact with those around them, their silence can be perceived as an act of aggression. Colleagues may feel rejected and anxious about what this person is thinking. This in itself can stimulate paranoid-type feelings. They might want to provoke a silent member, simply to elicit some sort of response. In brief, unspoken aggression can provoke attack; and silent fury can be a consequence of being tormented.

Is there a potential bully or victim in everyone?

Individuals brought up in a healthy, loving atmosphere are unlikely to bully another individual. Their childhood experience will have disposed them to making relationships which do not have aggression as a motivating factor. Equally, however, there are other individuals whose *modus vivendi* is to bully. Their childhood disposes them to set up situations in which they consciously or unconsciously intimidate others at work, at home, or both. It will stop only if they gain some insight into their motivation, or are actually removed from the particular environment altogether. However, the impulse to bully is present in everyone.

Between these two points is a spectrum of possibilities. Many people who, by and large, form good relationships will later admit to having had one difficult relationship with a colleague which, on reflection, they could consider to have been bullying, or to have contained bullying elements. These people are not bullies, but they realise that something which occurred within the relationship disturbs them. This is a hopeful sign, in that they have become aware of the impact of their actions. Similarly, they might also recognise occasions when they have been made to play the role of victim.

In the extreme but all too common instances of bullying that have been explored so far, the strength of the victim's response, their ability and persistence to fight back, depends to a large extent on the degree to which their self-esteem was nurtured in childhood. Those for whom the experience of bullying represents little more than a depressing confirmation of their childhood identity as a victim are – perhaps together with the bully – those most in need of professional help. The real victim is the individual stuck in the role of bully or victim. Both are in fact victims – of the inner conflicts which determine their psychological fate and imprison them.

Neil Crawford
1992

HELPING YOURSELF

It is important to discover that the way in which you handle staff is not helpful to either you or your organis-ation. This is the clearest signal that you need to look at yourself and try to establish why you behave as you do towards others. Identification with any of the following bullying styles can be the first step forward in the recovery process.

Recognition that you do any of the following:

- You insist that your way of doing things is always right.
- You tell people what needs to be done, then keep changing the instructions, perhaps in the hope that they will make mistakes.
- You give people tasks that you know they are incapable of achieving.
- You shout at your staff in order to get things done.
- You persistently pick on people and criticise them in front of others.

If your behaviour fits any of these descriptions think back and ask yourself if you have ever suffered the same treatment from anyone else. If so, how did it make you *feel*? Putting other people down may make you feel powerful, and in control, for the reasons that have already been explored in Chapter 6. Perhaps the *modus operandi* isn't always obvious. Here are some examples of ways in which a person can abuse a position of power by resorting to an unhealthy form of professional self-defence:

- Making life difficult for those who have the potential to do your job better than you.
- Keeping individuals in their place by blocking their promotion.
- Punishing others for being too competent by removing their responsibilities.
- Taking the credit for other people's ideas.
- Refusing requests for leave for no reason.
- Refusing to delegate because you feel you can't trust anyone but yourself.

If you recognise any of these traits in yourself, and are aware of the need to be in control of everything and everybody while you are at work, it will be helpful for you to discuss this use of authority. If you are afraid of losing the control you now have, and once again being over-powered by another person, these feelings may intensify when you are put under too much pressure.

- Perhaps you are afraid that if you fail to produce the results demanded by your organisation, you will be punished for not coming up to expectations?
- Could this fear stem from the constant criticism you received as a child, and the feeling that you never met with parental approval?
- Are you subjecting your employees to a similar experience?
- Do your actions reflect the influence of a previously aggressive boss?

These are all questions for which it is important to seek answers, once it is apparent that you may have a tendency to bully others.

The recovery process

When you have reached the point of self-acknowledgement, talking − in confidence − to those who can offer advice and understanding will help you to help yourself. Some of the options are listed below. You will find useful addresses, other suggestions, and a helpful reading list at the back of this book.

Some options

Employee counsellor
Personnel or welfare officer
Your GP
A counselling organisation

An organisation specialising in problems at work
Psychotherapy
Group therapy
Training in non-aggressive assertiveness

PART THREE

Seeking Solutions

Appreciation is a wonderful thing:
it makes what is excellent in others
belong to us as well.
Voltaire

9
Fighting Back

Courage can be just as infectious as fear.
Alice Miller, 'For Your Own Good'

Raising awareness is the primary aim of this book, to help all those involved to step back from this tangled and emotionally fraught experience and see it with a measure of detachment and objectivity. However, until organisations react in a positive way towards bullying at work, professional survival is down to three options. You leave to escape the problem altogether, accept what is happening because of financial commitments and your desire to work, or stand firm and fight.

On the evidence of experience, the first two options are, to say the least, unsatisfactory. Those who leave risk bearing a legacy of personal defeat. References based on the bully's vindictive assessment may raise awkward questions at subsequent job interviews. Those who stay and try to weather the storm are likely to face an escalation of the bullying, as well as a progressive erosion of both their self-confidence and their personal position. From this alone, it is clear that the third option, that of 'fighting back', offers the only real possibility of a solution to the complex and destructive problems posed by bullying in a work environment. This chapter examines some of the ways in which you as an individual can best set about defending yourself if you decide to make a formal complaint.

On a personal level, exploring and facing up to the reality of the situation is the first – and perhaps the most difficult – step in regaining a degree of control. It is the foundation on which you can begin to rebuild your battered self-esteem and eventually learn how to prevent the nightmare from recurring.

Clearly, though, these are long-term aims, and do not offer much comfort to those who are even now facing another week, another month, another year of bewildering demoralisation. Fortunately, there are more immediate practical steps which can be taken to launch an effective fight.

Blowing the whistle on a bully is not an easy option – not least because of the strain it quite clearly imposes in challenging a person who already makes you feel fearful. Anger at the injustice of something happening to you which is not your fault is, perhaps, the greatest motivator to fight back. But without a well-considered plan of attack, emotions can run riot, and nothing constructive is achieved except a sense of off-loading or release.

'A group of husbands were so angry at what this manager was doing to their wives who worked in the bank that they lay in wait to attack him as he returned to his car after work. That was the degree of lunacy going on.'

'In the end I wanted to kill the head. If someone had given me a gun I would have shot him. I have never felt the kind of loathing I felt for this man. I think the reason it got so bad was the frustration of my inability to deal with the situation, and also to come to terms with it. I couldn't do anything, so I felt impotent. I finally resorted to really petty things, like ringing him up in the middle of the night to wake him up. I let the tyres down on his car when he was at school late for a meeting so he would have trouble getting home. I took my keys and scratched the length of his new car. I'm not proud of having done any of these things, but it was sheer frustration that drove me to it because I felt there was nothing else I could do to try and get it to stop.'

These examples are by no means extreme. The powerlessness felt by these people is shared by the majority of adults who are bullied at work. Once they have failed in their attempts to change the bully's behaviour, or convince others in authority that one person is destroying staff morale, many leave their jobs while their sanity, at least, remains intact. It is a decision which, as we have already seen, leaves an unpleasant aftertaste, because it raises the question: Why should it be *me* that has to leave a job I like?

Anyone who has been subjected to this traumatic experience may have no wish to sacrifice career prospects, and financial security, by leaving to escape the bullying behaviour. It is worth remembering, therefore, that the combination of anger and frustration can be used as a constructive driving force to get round one of the fight under way.

It must also be remembered, however, that the obstacles which lie ahead require both staying power and stamina on the part of any individual. In many cases your opponent is not only the person accused of being a bully; it is also the organisation in which you work. If your employers regard your experiences as the normal state of play in any workplace, convincing them otherwise while ignorance prevails is likely to be a long-drawn-out procedure.

Even before you enter the confrontational ring, there are important factors to consider:

- Have you logged accounts of meetings or exchanges in which you or your professional competence were verbally attacked?
- Do your notes contain dates, times and locations of every slur on your character, or on contributions you

have made under your job description? (See also
'Asserting Yourself', p. 61)

- Have you retained copies of annual appraisals or letters
relating to your ability to do your job?
- Are you keeping copies of all memos sent by your boss?
Do you *know* your precise job description? Are your
responsibilities in line with it?
- If you are relatively new to the job, would senior
colleagues be prepared to support you and insist that
there is nothing wrong with your work?
- Are you feeling physically and emotionally well enough
to confront a person who has already affected your
health, and inflicted a punishing swipe on your self-
confidence?
- Are there others who have suffered as you have who
might be willing to support you?

The need for proof is essential because many organisations fail to recognise bullying, even when it is causing
serious disruption within their workforce. Once a label
was given to sexual harassment, on the other hand,
everyone involved with an allegation knew what they
were up against. Those on the receiving end knew what
term to use in order to make a complaint. Those who
had to address it found that it was something they could
no longer ignore.

Until bullying is recognised as a serious problem it is
important to be specific about the treatment to which you
have been persistently exposed; you need to have facts at
your fingertips. Otherwise, when you come to make a
complaint, your explanation of what has been causing
you to feel thoroughly undermined may well sound utterly
trivial.

Sarah's experience, which is not uncommon within the
teaching profession, illustrates the disadvantages of not
keeping a blow-by-blow account:

'It was my doctor who eventually advised me to take the matter to the Education Authority, but it was much more difficult than I had imagined. When I was relating what had been happening for two-and-a-half years, it all sounded so trivial. It seemed so childish and immature, as if the head was doing the kind of things that the pupils would do to each other. "He complained that I'd put my car in the wrong parking slot" . . . "He took my desk away" . . . "He shouts and stamps his feet" . . . "Other staff won't talk to the person whose turn it is to be bullied, in case he goes for them instead." The Education Authority's solution was to move me to another school, but because that meant demotion, and I'd worked very hard to achieve my promotion, I said I'd stay and try to persuade the head to agree to a fresh start.'

Sarah and her colleagues were eventually advised by their union to unite and stand up against this man, but by this time they were so divided, and so governed by fear, that such a solution was unthinkable. When he discovered that complaints had been made, his response highlighted one of the risks involved in attempting to fight back. He called Sarah into his office and started shouting, 'You've gone behind my back to your union; I'm going to make life hell for you if you don't do as I say.' Sarah was unable to shake off the fear of further recriminations, and even though she continued to stand up for herself, less than three years after her new boss took up his position, she had lost all belief in herself. She was physically and emotionally exhausted, and felt so impotent about her own inability to cope with the bullying that she finally gave up a job to which she was totally dedicated. It was Sarah's belief that she could never again face a classroom of schoolchildren. What is more, she was proved right.

Unfortunately, none of these teachers had recorded the proof that would have enabled them to complain more effectively, or in a more professional and detached way.

Consistent documented evidence produced by several members of the staff would have been difficult to refute.

Unions cannot act without proof either, and for those whose job it is to deal with complaints within an organisation, a diary or log of the story so far will aid any subsequent investigation. These people have to ascertain what is really going on, and it is worth considering the situation from their point of view as a way of focusing your own evidence. The question they are most likely to be asking themselves, for instance, is whether you, as the person making the complaint, might be doing so out of some sort of malice or revenge. If this person has been slapped down in the past, are they trying to get their own back? Are they simply getting at someone they can't work with? Most people at work have someone they bitch about, but in producing evidence about a real bully you must stick to the facts to avoid any hint of character assassination which might be misconstrued.

John, a sales manager:

'Time and time again she undermined our authority in front of junior members of staff, putting us down and trying to prove us wrong all the time. But because she was so good at putting herself across, and was seen to be so confident, when I complained I was more or less labelled a troublemaker. I got the feeling that the boss saw me as an ambitious young man who wanted to get rid of her in order to get promotion.'

Jacqueline, a schoolteacher:

'Whenever the governors were present he would be all sweetness and charm. Behind the doors of his office he would lose his temper and utter the most appalling comments. If you complained, it was your word against his. The governors wouldn't believe what they couldn't see for themselves, because in their eyes he was a kind, pleasant, and Christian man. Suggest anything to the contrary and you were seen as a

118

troublemaker out for some sort of professional revenge.'

Having established that the need for proof is imperative, the next obstacle is finding out whom to approach with the details of your experience, and its effects. You may prefer to make your initial approach, in confidence, to an employee counsellor if there is one operating within your place of work. Informal contact with a personnel department should give you the opportunity to explain the situation, and get a judgement on where to go next. If you are a member of a union, your representative should be in a position to seek action on your behalf.

Whether you decide to represent yourself as an individual, or to enlist other support, it is important to *call* it bullying. If you are aware that there are others being intimidated in this way, suggest that they might like to join together and make a complaint at the same time. There is always the risk that you may be accused of being an *agent provocateur*, but there is no doubt that when bullying at work is alleged, the larger the scale of the complaint, the more difficult it is to dismiss.

If it is your immediate boss or supervisor who is at the root of the problem, you may have to consider the 'grandfather principle' and go straight to the boss's boss. Whether or not your complaint is taken seriously will almost certainly depend on whom this person decides to believe – highlighting once again the need to keep an accurate account of what takes place over a period of time. At management level, of course, it may be impossible to establish in advance whether the person you have asked to consider your case is a personal friend of the bully. Experience shows that for this reason alone, any request for consideration of a complaint, especially one that is being handled without union support, should also go to the personnel department, to the Director of Personnel or Human Resources, and to their regional equivalent where this applies. To avoid any possibility of your complaint being overlooked at a lower level, copies of your letter should also go to any senior management executives, board members or, in the case of schools or hospitals, governors whom you believe you can trust. Be selective. Refrain from overpublicising your grievance at this stage to avoid being branded a troublemaker.

HELPING YOURSELF TO SURVIVE

The following experiences are intended to illustrate some of the difficulties you may encounter when you decide to stand up for yourself. At no time in their careers had these people met anyone who had treated them in such an unprofessional way. Finding themselves being bullied, without any just cause, they decided to fight back.

Kate (aged thirty-five)
The problem

A few months after she was appointed to a key role in an advisory service, Kate's boss, who had been with the organisation for twelve years, told her that he had grave concerns about her ability. He claimed that a client had made an official complaint relating to her work. His account of the incident was so different to what had really transpired, however, that she realised he was fabricating evidence against her. On this and other occasions, her own investigations proved that his accusations were unfounded. When he lied to other members of staff about her real reason for being off work, it was the last straw. She was incensed.

The action

'I'd already made one attempt to take him to task, by telephoning the regional director to complain about my boss's attempts to discredit me in a professional capacity. Then I discovered I'd been pipped at the post. The director said he was glad I'd called because he'd had my boss on to him expressing concern about my progress, saying he thought it should come under review. From our conversation there was no doubt that he believed my boss. Then I got a second chance. I had a photocopy of the sickness certificate which referred to my hospital operation, and although my boss had told everybody in the office he didn't think I was ill at all, I'd taken the precaution to send him one, too. This time I rang the regional director and asked him if he had seen the copy himself. It was obvious from what he said that my boss had lied to him. I said I hoped this would help him to realise that there were times when this man was not telling the truth. I also said that I had got to the point where I could no longer face what was happening at work, and could I please discuss the facts with personnel?

'From the moment I realised that my relationship at work with this man didn't feel right, I started making notes in a diary about where I'd been, whom I'd seen, and when. If he claimed something different, I'd also write that down. This made personnel wonder about my boss's behaviour because they knew there was nothing to be gained by my *not* telling the truth. What I didn't know at the time was that my boss socialised with the regional director outside office hours.'

The responses

It was suggested that Kate be transferred to headquarters in London, which she didn't want for a variety of personal reasons. Also, as she was the one being bullied, she didn't see why she should be the one to be moved. It had been established that she had been telling the truth all along, so it didn't seem fair. Kate then learnt, in a further meeting with her boss, that the director had been convinced that everything had been grossly exaggerated over 'a few silly little incidents'. The personnel manager told her that the next step was a meeting with her boss and the regional director, but when it took place, she felt as if she was facing a disciplinary situation. An approach to her union got a very different reception. No one needed convincing, they said, because Kate was by no means the first person to be on the telephone complaining about the behaviour of this individual. She was also warned, however, that despite union involvement, no marked improvement had ever been achieved.

The resolution

On this occasion the union were able to convince the regional director that there was room for doubt because of Kate's written record cataloguing her boss's lies. There were also witnesses to conversations who were now willing to support what she was saying. This meant that it was no longer a case of her word against his. Nevertheless, it was Kate who was subsequently moved to another office and her boss who remained. Since this episode in her life, Kate has gone on to qualify as a professional therapist. She is also involved in the setting up of Employee Assistance Programmes throughout the UK.

Kate, along with many people who find themselves being bullied, suffered the effects of severe stress – including depression – which caused her to require prolonged sick leave. Many people who have successfully fought back actually recommend taking a few days off work in order to recover from the latest onslaught, and to gain valuable thinking time. The chances are that if this is happening to you, your GP will already be aware of the cause and the effects. If not, put your doctor in the picture. Judging by the experience of men and women who have been bullied, many doctors are managing their stress by signing them off work for a few days, or even a few weeks, to provide them with a temporary recovery period. Officially, you may wish your GP to state the exact reason for your absence, or even contact your personnel department, in confidence, to discuss the specific cause. In the following example, a sickness certificate became an important piece of corroborating evidence.

Gwen (aged forty-five)
The problem

A year after joining a well-known charity as a secretary, Gwen challenged a defamatory statement made by her boss about another employee. From that day on, her boss, whenever she saw Gwen approaching, would turn her head the other way. She would insist that all Gwen's secretarial work be supervised, and then accused her of not using her initiative. Soon afterwards another woman was appointed as Gwen's new boss, and all responsibilities were taken away from Gwen. She was no longer allowed to answer the telephone or open incoming mail. She was rarely spoken to, and when she was, the conversation was peppered with belittling remarks. At departmental meetings, her previous boss would force an opinion out of her and then dismiss it at once as irrelevant. Gwen felt she was being 'treated in a way that any person in this country wouldn't even treat a dog, because if one came into the office, everyone would pat it and at least say "hello"'.

The action

'When I was threatened with disciplinary action for my work not coming up to scratch, I was able to throw the allegation back in their faces. I had already insisted that all instructions regarding my work were put into writing, so when it came to it, I had the proof that everything had been carried out as requested. I didn't respond immediately to the other forms of bullying, in the belief that you've got to let things ride for a while so you can be 100 per cent sure you've got a valid complaint. I even made a peacemaking move

123

by sending a note to my previous boss, suggesting that we got together for a coffee to sort out whatever it was that was the matter. Later, when I saw her open it, she looked at me, then glanced at the note and still didn't speak. I found that a *very* aggressive act. It was after this that I went straight to our chief personnel officer and gave her an account of what was happening within the department as a whole, and to me as an individual:

- How I wasn't being spoken to at all by my immediate boss.
- How I was being excluded.
- How colleagues' work was publicly rubbished and their credibility undermined as a result.

'I told her that having to work for someone who wasn't treating me as a human being was stripping away my self-respect, and asked how I could possibly work as part of a team under these conditions? It was reassuring to discover that I was the second person to approach her that day to make a complaint about the same two people. Her solution at this stage was to give me a couple of days off, but when I went downstairs to tell my boss that I was going home because I wasn't well, she told me she didn't think I was ill at all. She then demanded to know what I had been discussing in the personnel department. I was advised by personnel to make my complaint direct to my boss, and this I did. She then tried to cover up the true reason for our meeting by telling colleagues that I had really gone to her for counselling. She even tried to make out that I was mentally disturbed.

'My GP knew why I was so stressed at work, and if he thought it was getting too much for me, he'd find a reason to sign me off to relieve some of the pressure. After one period of sick leave, I took in a note which said my absence had been due to the atmosphere in the department. In a later sick note it actually named the person who was the source of my stress, but for some reason this wasn't picked up by personnel. Once I realised I was in a no-win situation, I decided to seek legal advice. My copy of the sick note naming my boss was considered a very important piece of evidence. I also found a colleague who was prepared to act as a witness and reveal that she had been specifically asked not to speak to me by my boss.'

The responses

Other secretaries were approached by Gwen's previous boss, who wanted to know if she was liked by other members of staff. She was, in fact, well liked, but the inference was that if people became too friendly with Gwen, they would risk putting their jobs on the line. Threatened with legal action, the organisation asked if it could have a couple of weeks to consider the case. Personnel suggested 'a nice, friendly, off-the-record' meeting to thrash out the problems between Gwen and her two senior colleagues.

Months later, with minimal notice, a day was set aside. Gwen, however, was not given a time, nor any indication of the format of the meeting. She had no opportunity to prepare her own case. As it turned out, minutes were formally taken, but no time was allowed to discuss the real issue. The meeting became a platform for the two bosses to level their complaints against Gwen, who did not feel that the personnel representative attempted to see fair play. However, her solicitor believed he had enough evidence to disprove their claims, and establish the damaging effects of working in this environment.

The resolution

The charity which employed Gwen made an intial offer, for an out-of-court settlement of £1,500. This was rejected by Gwen's solicitor, together with a reference which merely spelt out her job description and said nothing

125

about her own ability. The threat of a case of constructive dismissal finally pushed the figure up to £2,500, and once Gwen's reference had been improved, she was advised to accept. Soon afterwards, she was taken on as a highly specialised researcher in a legal organisation. In the next two years, six other members of staff left her previous place of employment.

Most of us are realistic enough to concede that there will almost certainly be someone at work whom we do not like. This does not preclude being civil, and using basic good manners to at least pass the time of day. In the case of a bully, however, you are likely to be up against a lack of social and interpersonal skills from the start.

Derek (aged fifty-eight)
The problem

For ten years Derek has attempted to stand up for himself, by appealing against allegations of insubordination while working as a civilian for the US Army. His troubles date back to the arrival of a new departmental supervisor at one British base. This man was like nobody else Derek had encountered in his entire career. Critical and ill-mannered, he frequently walked away in mid-conversation, refusing to acknowledge anyone else's ideas.

Given what he later discovered to be incorrect briefings, Derek would find himself accused of taking too long, or being inaccurate. Instead of returning the tasks to be reworked, the supervisor noted every error and even the date of the slightest mistake. In his previous places of employment, Derek's work had never come under criticism. What was happening to him now was described by a colleague as a psychological war of attrition. It was a situation he was not prepared to accept.

The action

'Once I realised I was beginning to think it was all my fault, I decided to talk it through with US personnel on the base. The moment I mentioned who I was complaining about, I was told it was an impossible situation, but because this guy knew what I was up against, I felt he understood the problem and it was a relief to have some sympathy. When I took my complaints to civilian personnel, I felt I was being asked set questions designed to extract particular answers. I didn't feel I could be honest with them. In fact I was extremely cautious with my replies in case they were used against me at some future date.

'I tried confronting the supervisor myself, in honest terms, in the genuine belief that because everyone has got a heart and feelings somewhere inside, this would work. When I suggested he was being unreasonable, he leant back in his chair with his hands behind his head, and with a Mona Lisa smile on his face told me that my work indicated otherwise. When I accused him of victimising me, the word got to him. I knew that guy meant business when he advised me against using it, because it's a legal word and he knew it would have to be proved. I did try the commander's 'open-door' policy, which means that if you've got a problem you can knock on his door and he'll see you pretty well right away. When it came to it, however, I found it very difficult to convince him that I wasn't trying to destroy this man, that I was just asking him to listen to what I had to say. Eventually, whenever there was another incident which slighted my professional competence, I put it in writing and kept a record. If I hadn't joined a union at this stage, my supervisor would probably have succeeded in getting me fired.'

The responses

Despite the fact that the supervisor was intensely disliked by his staff, Derek was instructed not to discuss his problems with other colleagues because this caused 'disharmony in the office'. After a letter to Derek marked 'Private' was opened by his boss, Derek made an official complaint. Although their offices were only a few feet apart, a memo was sent by the supervisor declaring that no private mail was to be allowed, and that all mail arriving in the office was subject to his authority. Official correspondence continued while the union confronted the charge of insubordination.

The resolution

When I interviewed Derek, his supervisor had stopped giving him work to do. Instead, he was trying to find minor tasks for himself, simply to show that at the end of each week he had achieved something. There had been no explanation as to why the man was behaving in this way. With more than six years still to complete before his retirement, Derek's wife felt he should stay put rather than leave a good job, with a good pension, and have to start somewhere else all over again. He had been informed by the base commander that he had no further right of appeal and was considering taking his complaint of being bullied to the European Court of Human Rights. Derek was determined to prove that he was in no way a different person at work from the person he had always been.

It may seem incredible that any individual has to sacrifice ten years of their life to try to convince others that they are still the same, dependable employee that the organisation originally appointed. But until the correct processes are in place to enable adults in employment to complain about being bullied – along with the added assurance that what they are doing is right – fighting back will continue to be an uphill struggle. Those who attempt to go the full ten rounds in the confrontational ring often do so in spite of an already shattered sense of self-esteem. They usually know, too, that when it comes to rank, it is whatever their boss says that is likely to be believed. Somehow, though, they find the physical and mental strength to become occupational trailblazers.

Suzanne (aged thirty-eight)
The problem

When a new line manager was promoted to Suzanne's department in the civil service, instructions were changed so often that nobody knew what they were supposed to be doing. When something went wrong it was always assumed it was their fault, never his. He always told them that they had misunderstood. He also succeeded in disguising his lack of organisation from his own boss by giving his staff unreasonable deadlines. He used Suzanne's annual report to downgrade aspects of her personality and management ability that had previously merited high marks. In an overall assessment, these lower marks were likely to affect her promotion prospects and performance-related pay. She worried that no independent body looking at her personal file in the future would realise that these alterations were unjustified. When Suzanne was moved away from her colleagues to the other end of the room in which she worked, it was the culmination of a series of incidents which were gradually destroying her sense of self. It led to her resignation, but a few days later she retracted her notice, in the hope that somebody would at last listen.

The action

Not for the first time Suzanne applied for a move to another branch, but was refused. She then approached her second line manager, who said his door was always open [Suzanne says the staff would add 'but my ears are always shut!']. It became clear, however, that he had already asked her boss for his version of events and was clearly on his side when he asked for hers. The man interrupted her throughout the interview and then announced that he felt there had been no mismanagement. Suzanne was told to bury her grievance and warned that her boss would be fully backed if she continued with her complaint. It was then that she decided to write a long and detailed account of everything that had happened to her at work to present to personnel. Although she had received an informal warning relating to poor performance, everything she now took on was done faultlessly and at top speed. She even went over things twice to make sure she met and exceeded all her schedules. Suzanne became obsessed with her grievance report, which took up all her spare time. Five months later, she handed it to the Head of Personnel and then had to take time off because of her state of exhaustion.

The responses

Suzanne was immediately transferred to another branch. However, she felt unable to cope with the additional stress of adapting to new ways of working. Her GP told her that she must have a month off work. When she did join the new branch, she was reassured to find a supportive environment, but she had become so used to her previous boss finding fault with everything she did that her confidence was severely affected. The long wait for a response to her complaint was agonising. By the time it arrived, the Head of Personnel had moved on and his replacement dismissed the case. Suzanne's only option was to refer it to Personnel Management, which she did two months later after further constructing her case. After another two months a letter arrived apologising for the delay. It confirmed that her case was under investigation. Two months after that, she was invited to a meeting a fortnight later to discuss her grievance, with her husband present if she so wished.

The resolution

It was accepted that Suzanne's low performance mark partly resulted from undue pressure from her first line manager, and that he had allowed a poor working relationship to develop. It was also established that he had given her no advance warning of a lowered mark to allow her to improve. Personnel Management ruled that the record of informal warning should be deleted from Suzanne's file, and that her low mark would be disregarded for pay and promotion purposes. None of her witnesses was interviewed because she was finally believed. It was felt that no one would have persisted with complaints for two years without good cause. But the exhausting process had taken its toll. Suzanne was suffering from depression and other stress-related reactions, but she was determined to get her life in order again. Relaxation therapy was crucial to her recovery, but it was her husband's emotional support throughout that proved invaluable. Six months later she was fit enough to return to work.

The legal option

In the absence of any positive response which fails to resolve the situation, resignation is always a last resort if you no longer feel able to stay in your job. But you may be able to prove to an industrial tribunal that you felt compelled to resign because of the way you were being treated. Provided you have been employed there for no less than two years, and you have logged, in detail, how, when and where you believe you have been bullied, you may have a sound case of 'constructive dismissal' against your organisation.

It is the task of a tribunal, therefore, to establish whether you had good grounds for walking out because you could no longer stand the behaviour to which you were being subjected.

The following paragraph is an extract from the Employment Law Supplement 46, supplied by Incomes Data Services:

131

'Breaking the camel's back'

Problems sometimes arise as to whether the final incident resulting in an employee's resignation was really serious enough to justify his departure. Most of the time, of course, the 'last straw' itself will be a relatively major breach. In case CO1T 1477/770 a tribunal held that a hotel manager over the course of a year had terrorised a fifty-three-year-old waitress by singling her out for unfair treatment and regularly losing his temper with her in an unfair manner. C finally resigned when the manager yelled obscenities and threw a chair at her because she was slightly late in preparing some coffee. This was 'not a straw, but a haystack', the tribunal said, and would probably have entitled C to leave irrespective of earlier incidents.

In cases of unfair dismissal, tribunals are interested in *how* the person was dismissed, not *why*. In other words, they examine whether or not the correct procedures were carried out by the employer. A request for an acceptable reference can be built into a winning claim. Compensation varies, but the ceiling is little more than £10,000. It is a figure which comes up for review every April.

If you need advice about taking your case to an industrial tribunal, where do you go?

Any Citizens' Advice Bureau or your local Job Centre. Here, a designated officer will explain the procedure and should be able to offer the free Department of Employment leaflets relating to industrial tribunals and claims for compensation. Legal Aid is available only for advice, not for legal representation, but there is nothing to prevent you from presenting your own case.

Industrial tribunals are open to the public, and to the press, which may encourage an employer to settle out of court in preference to the potential risk of bad publicity. The risk to the individual is the possibility of being labelled a troublemaker. However, Helen's experience (see Chapter 3) suggests that any such stigma is unlikely if the applicant is quite open about the reasons for taking their case to court.

Remembering what to do

- Keep a written record of incidents: dates and details of all threatening exchanges, and of any disparaging comments about your character or personal competence. Whenever possible, write these down immediately afterwards while they are still fresh in your mind.
- Once you have written proof about what has been happening to you at work, send the bully a memo drawing attention to the reaction you received. Any reply will add to your evidence, as will a refusal to respond. Keep copies of all correspondence, previous appraisals or annual reports.
- Ask for the support of colleagues who may have witnessed any of the incidents, even if this is in writing and anonymous in the first instance.
- Take your evidence to a personnel manager, senior colleagues and your trade-union representative if appropriate. Request confidentiality.
- Try to keep calm, but don't battle on if you are afraid of losing control. Sick leave need not be a sign of weakness; it can be a strategy to take time over decisions about what to do next.
- (See also the *Helping Yourself* section in Chapter 5)

10
Getting It Right

A policy of good human relations at work is not about jobs, it is about people.
Marcus Sieff *On Management: The Marks & Spencer Way*

It is estimated that since the mid 1950s time off work with stress-related illness has increased by 500 per cent and now costs industry hundreds of millions of pounds a year. In America, the Bureau of National Affairs, which produced a special report in 1990 called *Violence and Stress: The Work/Family Connection*, has stated that US businesses are losing five to six billion dollars a year in decreased productivity alone. It blames the real or perceived abuse of employees.

In November 1991, John Banham, then Director-General of the Confederation of British Industry, spoke out at a conference on the mental health of employees and made it clear that British business needed to 'make optimal use of all its assets including, and most especially, its people'. A survey carried out in 1991 by the CBI, in association with the Department of Health, revealed that thirty times as many working days are lost through mental illness as are lost through industrial disputes. Although there can be other reasons for stress-related illness, no one in British industry has made a direct link with the problem of bullying at work, despite the clear message from the CBI that a healthy and confident workforce is critical to the success of any organisation. Ironically, the following extract illustrates how long problems have been allowed to linger.

The Daily Telegraph, 9 September 1971
MANAGEMENT BLAMED FOR RISING TOLL OF MENTAL ILLNESS
by John Kemp, Social Services Correspondent

Mental illness has grown to such proportions that it now causes more lost working days than strikes, go-slows, influenza or the common cold, it was reported yesterday.

Mr David Ennals, director of the Mind campaign for the National Association for Mental Health, said much of the blame was due to management.

It created situations of stress for workers. Inadequately trained managements who failed to understand the importance of job satisfaction or consulting workers might be responsible for the 'English disease' of absenteeism, sickness absence, clock-watching, apathetic performance, low productivity and a failure to meet delivery dates.

Recent evidence showed mental illness had resulted in the loss of more than 36 million working days each year, though the real figure might be much higher – perhaps 50 million days, which is five times last year's figures for strikes.

A team of mental health and industrial health experts in a report for the Association to be submitted to Lord Robens' committee on safety and health at work argues that some management decisions, made without knowledge or understanding of the psychological needs of employees, might be a direct cause of stress and mental health.

The report highlights four danger points:

1. Overpromotion could result in a breakdown because a man was trying to deal with responsibilities beyond his capacity.
2. Underwork – agreeable for a time but led to dissatisfaction, demoralisation and frequent spells of absence for minor complaints.
3. Poor job definition. If a man was not sure about the requirements of his job or to whom he was responsible it might become a major strain.
4. Lack of consultation and communication.

The key to mental health was job satisfaction, says the report.

Men and women have clearly suffered too long the arrogance of their employers. Such major clues to getting it right were provided in the above piece of reporting that – in the light of the many experiences recounted in this book – it is inexcusable that the danger points, so accurately identified, failed to set a more stable pattern for the future.

Today, consultation and communication are buzz words in any organisation which recognises that the people it employs are its greatest resource. In their wisdom, employers have equated a happy and contented workforce with the ability to meet a competitive challenge and the financial benefits which result. In other words, they have realised the importance of putting people before profit.

Prevention is part of the cure. However, where the bottom-line culture is everything for profit, not people, and top managers applaud ambitious drive and aggressive decision-makers, it is the people who are often treated badly in the process. Yet in the 1991 CBI survey, nine out of ten companies considered the mental health of their employees to be vital to the competitiveness of the UK. More than 50 per cent of companies even said they understood the causes and effects of mental illness. Why, then, is bullying in the workplace – which frequently causes mild to severe depression, as well as many other stress-related illnesses – a problem that is not being properly addressed?

Going to work to be respected by people at all levels, and valued as a member of the community, should not require revolutionary tactics on the part of an employee. Strong leadership which refuses to endorse a bullying style is a decision that should be high on the agenda of any organisation which seeks to provide a place in which people enjoy working. Failure to do so is money down the drain. What is the point of huge investments in training programmes if people leave their jobs to escape this unwarranted aggression, or bullies themselves are not helped to unlearn behaviour that has established bad habits?

Those at the top must learn a new concept of responsibility towards their employees, and an understanding that bullying is symptomatic of something wrong within the organisation. Until this is achieved, personnel departments, counsellors and union officials will continue to pick up the pieces. There is, for example, a tendency among those who are subjected to this sort of aggressive treatment to become alienated from the organisation in which they work. When it is sensed that the organisation doesn't care about what happens to the individual, there is a feeling of 'why the hell should *we* care about the organisation'?

One of the most important ground rules to be established by any personnel department is that people must feel safe to come forward and make a complaint about being bullied. First, however, there must be a clear organisational structure so that employees know to whom they can turn to resolve the situation. They must also know that a complaint of this nature will be taken seriously – either through a clear statement in a staff manual or company handbook, or on posters displayed in areas used by employees at all levels, e.g.: Bullying and unwarranted aggression at work is a problem that this organisation recognises. It is one that it does not endorse, and if it is experienced by any employee, it will offer help and support for any individual.

This was the guideline conceived by Jane, the Director of Human Resources at the academic establishment mentioned in Chapter 5, for which Nick worked. It followed a sequence of events following an official complaint which concerned eight men, all members of NALGO – the National Association of Local Government Officers – and a senior member of the academic staff. Jane believes it was made against a background of belief that nothing would be done. She admits that as far as she was concerned, a complaint of this nature presented an entirely new concept, one that she had never had to deal with before in a career spanning twenty years in personnel.

The following is an extract from the official letter of complaint sent in 1991 to Jane, and three other members of senior management, by the two NALGO stewards.

Subject: Conditions of work

The NALGO Executive received a formal request for help yesterday to counter the bullying and harassment by an academic member of staff, [named here].

NALGO consequently has held a meeting of all members today at which the following was expressed.

All members agreed that there is an atmosphere of fear at —

Members are distressed and complain of their confidence being destroyed. Their working relationship with each other, with students and with other academic members of staff have all been detrimentally affected. People are afraid to talk to each other whether Mr — is on or off site.

Work is being directly affected, stress-related illness, they believe, has increased. They now dread going to work.

We are writing to you to ask for urgent help to resolve this intolerable situation. As you can imagine NALGO is treating this matter very seriously and will not want to delay in taking further action if no progress is made by more formal means.

The role of personnel is to take on board any issue raised by any individual within an organisation, at whatever level, and try to find an effective solution. The difficulty which arises is ascertaining the truth behind the allegations, while at the same time maintaining a balance between both sides – that of the employee and that of the organisation. This was Jane's experience as Director of Human Resources.

True or false?

'It was not a question of siding with the employees, even though there were eight of them. It was a case of listening to all the parties involved on a no-threat basis, although this was difficult because I knew that ultimately I might have to implement the disciplinary procedure. Once I met these men I was quite shocked by their physical and emotional state. I certainly had no doubts about proving that there was a problem, because of the number of people involved. No one denied what was going on and I had access to all the evidence I required. The only question mark hung over the degree of effect the bullying was having. Because I had only been with the institution for a few months at this point, I decided to inspect the records of this particular department. They showed a great deal of movement of staff, including sideways moves, all of which had taken place in the three years since the man accused of bullying joined the establishment at a very senior level. There was now not one person left in the department who had been teaching there when he arrived, and although that could have been coincidence, there was no escaping the fact that no one wanted to work in this particular section, and that included most of the students. Also, what had previously been a successful and popular department was now a totally devastated area. I think the allegations had an even greater impact on me because those complaining were all men between twenty-six and forty. It certainly knocked the "big boys don't cry" stereotype.'

The initial response of union colleagues to Nick's suggestion that he was being bullied by his immediate boss was, as explained in Chapter 5, one of ridicule. Three years later, when he *called* it 'bullying', the same group of people were stunned and saw it as a genuine cry for help from the colleague. The two stewards who represented the NALGO members recall their side of the story:

139

'When we met the group what they told us was very fundamental. He's a horrible man . . . he treats us badly . . . it's changed the whole atmosphere. Because it sounded so trivial, we'd say "Hasn't he hit you?" almost wanting him to have done something awful. Then we could say gross misconduct, you're suspended, you're out. As they talked, we got the feeling it was affecting the whole site, including the students. We asked the men to start keeping a log of incidents which occurred, and it was agreed that a letter should go to personnel as a show of solidarity, with union support. Meanwhile, it was certainly helpful to have a label that everybody understood because it encapsulated what had been happening. When we received a reply, it was important for us to hear that we were doing the right thing by making a complaint. It also reinforced that the problem was being recognised. During this time we kept in close contact with personnel, and with NATFHE [National Association of Teachers in Further and Higher Education], which was representing the lecturer accused of being a bully. There was a lot of anxiety surrounding the possibility of facing the bully across a table if it came to a disciplinary hearing. The men were fearful that he would start attacking them again, and because they felt their complaints would sound so trivial, they were convinced that he would be the one to be believed. We had awful meetings about where they would sit, and who would read out their statements. They were like frightened schoolchildren.

'At no time would management suspend this man, even when he'd been accused of bullying others, yet it would have helped our members enormously if this person had been temporarily removed. It would have helped them to feel safer, having made their complaint, until the result of the internal inquiry. It shocked us to think that this had been going on for three years, yet people were being so civilised about it, as if it was a temporary aberration.'

The dilemma

'Handling this from the personnel side wasn't easy. You can assure confidentiality to reduce the level of fear being experienced by anyone who says they have been bullied, but for a disciplinary procedure, witnesses are required to provide evidence. Also, while you may have tremendous sympathy for anyone who has suffered, you have to respect justice for the accused person. It is fraught with difficulties all round. In a sense I had to prejudge. To select the appropriate person to hear the case I had to determine, in advance, the level of misconduct. If it was a case of gross misconduct, for example, whoever was appointed had to have the power to dismiss.'

How did others see this man? How did he see himself? What role did the institution itself play in endorsing his personal style?

The accused

The NATFHE representative:

'His perception of himself was entirely different to the way in which he was seen by those who were complaining of being bullied. Here was a lecturer being forceful in an academic sense, with a character that tended to roll over other people. This could have been seen as not leaving space for anybody in a subordinate position within the organisation. Add to that a structure in which neither the terms of job definitions, nor the functioning of the hierarchy, is particularly well defined. In this environment, a person who is very assertive and strong, perhaps in a nebulous way, is given a great deal of licence.'

The NALGO representatives:

'He wanted control over everybody else's lives. He had an extremely poor record of interpersonal relationships with everyone we knew about. We were told that reports had been written about his behaviour a long time before, telling the organisation what was going on. Those from fellow academics were sent on a very professional basis, suggesting that this person shouldn't be teaching students. Nothing was done, as if the problem would somehow go away.'

The Director of Human Resources:

'Whether he worked with or over other people, none of his relationships appeared to work out satisfactorily. In one way I was fearful of meeting him because someone had said: for goodness' sake don't let him between you and the door, make sure you have another person present. When it came to it, he was charming, and full of personality, although I could feel that all the barriers were up. He had his union representative with him, but because I could see he was so uptight, I spent five minutes chatting in general terms and made sure I sat near him. I also used an easy, friendly approach. Despite that, he was shaking and clearly very nervous, yet I now understand that no one had ever seen him like that. When I confronted him with the effects his behaviour had been having, one of his responses was: "I'm accused of pointing at people. I *never* point at people when I talk". He was pointing at me in just the way that had been described as he said this.'

How it was resolved

Following this one meeting, the NATFHE representative advised his member that to carry on in his present job would, under the circumstances, make his position untenable. He resigned. Although the disciplinary hearing never took place, personnel had decided that this man had to be removed because of the profound effect he was having on the mental health of the eight men who had made a formal complaint. The accused man's new employers never took up a reference. A job was offered on his academic reputation alone.

Lessons learnt

- The institution decided that bullying at work was an issue. It offered its support to personnel in planning clear complaints procedures for all members of staff – Director of Human Resources
- It was important to set patterns to establish what was considered reasonable behaviour – NATFHE
- There should be a clearly understood disciplinary code. Everyone, at whatever level, must be made aware that there is the opportunity for some redress if they feel they are being bullied – NALGO

Once there is acknowledgement that serious difficulties are being experienced within its walls, these are some of the clearest warning signs to any organisation that, in any one department, it could have a problem with bullying at work:

- High staff turnover
- Absenteeism
- Regular or prolonged sickness absence
- Staff looking tense or troubled
- A change in atmosphere

143

- Reduced productivity
- Less concern with quality
- Low morale
- Loss of initiative
- Lack of creative input

The physical and emotional symptoms experienced by those being bullied listed on page 63 are also important clues for anyone trying to identify what might be wrong. Asking the right questions of anyone making a complaint will not only establish the effects, if they are being bullied, it will also pinpoint when a change in the workplace occurred.

Ask yourself:

- Has there been a change at the head of this organisation?
- Is the person complaining of being bullied working under a new boss?
- Have they recently joined this organisation?
- Is an employee who was previously considered perfectly reliable now being accused of poor performance?
- Are an increasing number of dismissals being recommended by a new boss?

If the answer to any of these questions is 'yes', check past records and references. Look for changes between then and what you are now being told. Is it a case of a bully trying to get rid of the competition? Is this individual no longer able to work effectively because of ever-changing objectives? Do staff seem less confident, dispirited, depressed?

One of the problems faced by the personnel department at the academic establishment for which Nick worked came when it was dealing with subsequent complaints of bullying. Because these were made by individuals, and because the accounts given were about behaviour that 'sounded as it if came under the heading of intimidation', the Director of Human Resources admits that, initially, she found the claims unconvincing:

> 'There is a scale from the mildest form of intimidation, which is none the less disturbing, to the other end where the fear is just so severe that you only have to look at the faces to see the effects. For me the difficulty is: which part of the scale is this new problem at? At the extreme end it is very easy to address. I am also aware, however, that not only do the milder forms have similar physical effects, these cases can move up the scale and become very severe.'

It is essential, therefore, to keep a constant watch for the psychological well-being of all staff. It is also crucial to understand the psychology of group phenomena. Knowing what to look for, and why, should make it possible to take pre-emptive measures by identifying anyone who is using a bullying style. Failure to do so will only exacerbate the situation. Unless a firm line is taken against this type of behaviour, at an early stage, the bully will see inaction as confirmation that his or her way of using authority is not only entirely appropriate, but acceptable. This is not, however, a recommendation for witch-hunt assessments, but for a subtle piece of investigation to help those on all sides.

Once this problem has been identified, there is a further dilemma. Should it mean a transfer for the person being bullied, or must the bully be moved elsewhere? It must be remembered that where bullying has occurred within an organisation, those affected will remain fearful, even after the situation has been fully resolved, if the bully remains. Until their confidence has been rebuilt, with counselling support, normality will not be restored. It is also clear, from some of the experiences related in earlier chapters, that these people feel a tremendous sense of injustice if they are the ones to be moved, through no apparent fault of their own, while the bully remains. So what is the solution? Helping the bully to change within the organisation will be explored in Chapter 12, although in the case of a sadistic bully, this is likely to be an unrealistic expectation. Without help, however, moving the bully to another department, another branch or another area is merely moving the problem elsewhere.

The following difficulties were encountered when a senior manager, believed to have caused distress in his previous workplace, took up a new post within one of Britain's more recently privatised industries. Soon after his arrival, staff in one department were bewildered by his attitude as their competence and integrity was persistently attacked.

The new boss

Suddenly, accusations of underperformance, poor communication, inability to get on with others, failure to operate as a team, taking sick leave too often were being levelled at staff. It was even suggested that two of the employees suffered from personality disorders – an allegation that was disproved by a medical expert by whom they were examined at a later date.

The staff knew that there had been no change in either their attitude or their ability to do the job. They were aware that if there had been, the matter would have been raised by previous managers. While several of them came under constant criticism, a newer colleague was never accused of underperformance, despite the fact that he was viewed by the rest of the department as incompetent. If the manager was asked to justify why he felt others were underperforming, he failed to come up with an explanation, even when pressed. When three of the women in the department got tired of being constantly undermined and demeaned by this man, both in public and in private, they approached their NALGO representative to make a formal complaint.

The grievance

- Fails to provide adequate leadership by not making his intentions or requirements clear.
- Fails to ensure that all staff were adequately trained when new equipment was installed.
- Changes conditions of work without consultation or agreement.
- Continually puts staff under stress by questioning their attitude to work.
- Disputes all medical reasons for absence, even when evidence is provided by the doctor concerned.
- Has made no attempt to instil team spirit within the department, despite the content of their boss's recent memorandum on 'People Management'. ['Managers can only expect the response from staff they want if they treat them as mature adults and trust them.']

Unlike the formal complaint put to the academic establishment by the same union, this complaint did not include the word bullying. It would almost certainly not have occurred to either the branch members or their representative that this was the appropriate word to describe exactly what was going on. Information about the physical and emotional effects being experienced by these women would have provided some necessary clues. However, direct contact with someone, at the same level as their immediate boss in personnel, was deemed unsatisfactory by these employees. It was known that the two men had previously worked together, and there was a suspicion – unfounded or not – that he was bound to take sides.

The result

Two days after the grievance hearing, the three women received written confirmation that their allegation against

147

their boss had been dismissed. The letter also confirmed support for this man's management, considering it 'both firm and fair, as reflected by his success in previous posts'. Expressing concern that they found working in the situation unacceptable and stressful, the manager who heard their grievance said he believed that relationships had irretrievably broken down. It was felt to be in their best interests that they should be urgently redeployed.

The aftermath

One woman left her job. Before their redeployment, the remaining two were no longer allowed to sit together. Their boss took every opportunity to inform them that they did not understand the severity of making such allegations. The union insisted that there would be no more trouble. In the case of one woman, the confrontations continued. Both were moved to posts that appeared to be newly created, yet they received nothing in writing to confirm that these jobs were officially part of the staffing structure. Following independent advice, they asked their union to ratify the posts, and their job descriptions, as quickly as possible. When one of the women started her new job in a different department, there were no introductions. She later discovered that colleagues had been told that there was nobody working in the room she occupied, and that the new team was being built up from scratch. The two women remained because they knew it would be impossible to find jobs requiring their specialist skills, in the same city, at the same level of pay. Neither of them wished to leave the area. Less than a year after their grievance hearing, their previous boss was promoted into another post within the same organisation, but in a different establishment. He became responsible for more than a hundred employees.

* * *

One issue raised by this story is that of impartiality. Maintaining a friendly attitude, but at a distance, is the only feasible stance for anyone in a personnel role. This is how it has been described by Tim, who has reached the top of his profession:

'You often hear about the loneliness of the chief executive. The same has to apply to people in personnel, and it can be a very isolating existence. Friendships within the organisation make it too difficult to take an objective view when other people are involved, especially in the event of a disciplinary situation. After all, the personnel role is about balancing the needs of all employees, as well as the responsibility it has to the organisation itself.'

There is no doubt that many of those in a personnel role are unable to take the strong line they would like to take in certain situations because of the attitude of those above. In a case of bullying, for example, it might prove impossible to convince a senior manager in an aggressively run organisation that those making the complaint were anything more than a bunch of wimps. Personnel managers will need to draw on all their counselling and intervention skills to get the message across. Indeed, comprehensive training in these skills is essential.

Without the power, or permission, to offer proper redress, taking matters into their own hands would merely risk putting their own jobs on the line. For this reason alone, unions, where recognised, have a strong role to play in helping to seek justice for those whose cases may otherwise not be fairly considered.

Current challenges under the Health and Safety at Work Act 1974 include organisations' responsibility for the security of their employees. Issue has already been taken with cases of sexual harassment and racial discrimination. With the introduction of European directives covering the rights of workers, it is to be hoped that employers may well be exposed to further legislative requirements to add to their existing duty of care, and that employees will be adequately protected from bullying at work, and the grievous mental harm it can cause.

Until organisations look inward, and implement some self-analysis, turbulent undercurrents will, in many cases, continue to create a climate of discontent. Bullying may well be at the source of underlying distress, but until such time as the reasons for its occurrence are fully explored, these can be further clues to its existence:

Appraisals

1. The lowering of previously higher marks or grades.
2. A conflicting assessment of personal qualities compared with earlier appraisals.

As the broader purpose of an appraisal is to help build the relationship between boss and subordinate, these are clear warning signs that this is beginning to break down.

If there are no obvious reasons for a change in standard of behaviour, or quality of performance, then it is important to investigate. Where the completed appraisal requires the signature of the boss's immediate superior, it would be helpful, in all cases, if this person could first check through the previous report, and then be prepared to make an accurate comparison. In cases where the boss is being totally unfair, some special measure must be taken to ensure that what is written is a factual record, as seen by the organisation.

References

Employers who decide to get rid of a bullying boss may resort to the schoolteacher principle and despatch them with a reference that bears little relation to their performance, on a personal level, within the workplace. If doubts do arise once they are established in a new post, a call by personnel to their previous employer is likely to prove far more useful than a written record. Ideally, any queries should be followed up at the selection stage, after references have been checked against interview to see what might have been hedged, or is actually missing. One of the greatest burdens to impose on a bully – or a potential bully – is to enable them to step above their ability and not be able to cope with the subsequent demands.

Stress audits

Where these are carried out, they provide valuable information from employees within the organisation about management style. If there is a fundamental problem with rapid staff turnover and poor performance – which in normal circumstances does not exist – this is the type of information which will be picked up as a result of stress audits. The data collected can also pinpoint an area where a manager's performance is leading to absenteeism and ill health. These indications that there is a critical problem within an organisation may require outside help to be brought in to deal effectively with the overall source of the stress.

Exit interviews

One of the frustrations facing personnel is finding out about a problem after notice has been given. By this time, the situation may be irrevocable – at least for the individual who has decided to resign. A thorough, confidential exit interview carried out by a personnel officer will serve two important purposes:

1. It will give the employee an important opportunity to unburden stifled feelings of anger and resentment that have been building up for some time.
2. It will provide valuable information about examples of unseen aggression which can be remedied to protect those who remain.

11
Organisational Responsibility

To see what is right and not to do it
is want of courage.
Confucius

It is vital to understand that bullying is a symptom. It is a manifestation of conflicts within an individual, or within an organisation, but dealing with it head on, as if it were the whole problem, will fail to get at the roots. In the interests of the long-term understanding of all concerned, there must be a capacity to tease out the factors behind aggression.

It may be difficult to take on board the fact that many people bring the legacy of their past to work, and take it out on those they work with. However, unless this fact is understood, much of the behaviour that takes place at work will simply not make sense.

It can be argued, of course, that it is not the aim of an organisation to understand itself. Every organisation has a task, and the people in it are primarily concerned with the fulfilment of that task. It does not exist to further the understanding of its workforce, except in relation to getting the job done. After all, the livelihood of the organisation depends on it fulfilling its obligations.

This persuasive argument – that we concern ourselves with what we do, not how we are – can seem convincing – except when the conflicts in human relations interfere with, or impede, the primary task.

Healthy organisations, on the other hand, can be identified by the way in which they marry the task with the needs of employees. It is not surprising that in a hostile, frightened organisation the worst sides of an individual will be brought to the surface. Conversely, while a concerned, humane workplace may not be paradise, it is more likely to foster good relations. In this type of environment, bullying could not flourish because it would be unacceptable.

However, because of its association with behaviour that may have taken place at school, many people consider that bullying is a characteristic that is not too serious, even though it is unpleasant. In fact the gradations of aggression, which range from an irritated response to outright fury, are innumerable. It also follows, however, that the line where common tensions end and unacceptable bullying begins is inevitably blurred. Common tension is a misleading concept. It assumes that problematic relationships in the workplace are inevitable, supporting the notion that such difficulties are not only lived with, but also acceptable.

The ethos of an organisation

Where does firm management end and bullying begin? Much has been written about management style, and it is a continuing debate. But observation has taught me that there is a gap between how organisations describe their management, and what they actually do in practice. It is not enough to say, 'We work democratically here'. One starting point to help organisations understand themselves is an honest appraisal of how they work. This may well contrast with how they would like to see themselves.

Jerry, a shop steward, considers the problem from another angle. He draws on his experience of dealing with the blurred boundary:

'People in subordinate positions may find it difficult in the first instance to recognise that certain lines have

153

been overstepped. And in the second instance, knowing what the hell to do about it if the institution is loosely structured. Patterns of behaviour then begin to develop that are self-perpetuating, and if there is weakly defined management, they don't get challenged from within. When problems arise, they tend to fester rather than be raised and addressed at an early stage. It becomes more difficult for people who feel bullied to express it because they feel intimidated by it. And for those who bully, it becomes confirmatory that what they are doing is perfectly right and proper within their job.'

It is easy to say 'deal with problems as they arise'. This is, in fact, a difficult proposition. It assumes that those within the workplace can spot what is going on, and know how to approach the problems.

Some organisations thrive on internal competition, the bounds of which are difficult to draw. Among those in which aggressive marketing predominates, 'bullying' members of a team is accepted practice. It may well be labelled motivation or cajoling, or perceived as 'necessary pressure': an acceptable means of 'getting the best out of them'.

The pressure for results is increased where earnings are linked to team performance. If one member is not pulling their weight, they are considered fair game for criticism and can find a great deal of anger coming their way. In this respect, malicious teasing is also considered acceptable within organisations, and employees would be frowned on if they objected. Yet persistent teasing can not only be very upsetting, it can mask enormous aggression.

The dilemma is deciding what is acceptable practice in the workplace. David, a personnel director, gives a case in point:

'He's been with us for ten years, and although there have been numerous complaints about him, the reason

154

it hasn't been dealt with is that people will come to accept certain stereotypical characters. A newsroom is an environment of pressure and noise, and the staff tolerate the news editor who shouts at everybody to get things done. While it wasn't affecting our outside relationships, it didn't matter so much. But since he's had a more public profile, and staff have been bawled at in front of clients, we've had to step in and challenge his behaviour before it undermined our credibility as a company.'

A critical criterion in this company was the risk to its image and, taken to an extreme, people's jobs. It was only when relationships outside the company were at risk that action was taken. Again and again, it is possible to see organisations tolerating behaviour which becomes acceptable at some level to those within. For this reason, new employees, who are not organisation-weary, can find themselves in a complaining role, deeply affected by their experience. It can be very instructive to listen to new recruits to gather a sense of what is really going on.

The reflections of the personnel director on what he learnt from the bully are also instructive:

'He's been under stress at home for many years; therefore, when as a company we know a person is under pressure at home, I wonder whether we should think more carefully about putting a person like this in a pressurised role at work as well, especially if it manifests itself in this type of conduct.'

Although it seems sensible to take the home life of an individual into account, some would argue that what takes place at home has nothing to do with the organisation. Others would insist on the opposite. However, until organisations understand that the split is artificial, and the two are in fact intertwined, they will continue to

155

expect individuals to perform a role without understanding either the person or the performance.

Where a difficulty is related to a problem at home, it becomes a problem for the organisation once work – or working relationships – become deeply affected by the individual's actions. The following factors need to be considered:

- The persistency and extent of a person's aggression.
- Whether they are aware of the impact of their actions on others.
- If they feel any guilt or concern when they upset people at work.

It is insufficient, however, to consider individuals alone. Where symptoms of organisational ill health are in evidence, intervention is required. By organisational ill health, I mean any behaviour which results in poor management, inefficiency, high staff turnover and an inability to develop full potential.

Responsibility and understanding

When human relations at work get out of hand, there is often a clearly designated individual to help pick up the pieces. Where there is no one willing to take responsibility, the conduct associated with a bully can carry on unabated and unchecked. In fact, even where there *is* a named individual, such as a personnel director or human resources manager, there is no guarantee that they will have the power, understanding or will to work through the problems which arise. After all, the presence of a referee in a football match does not ensure that trouble will not take place. However, there are many instances where the skills of personnel professionals enable the organisation to identify and resolve issues to its benefit – in efficiency, and in job satisfaction in particular.

156

In a large organisation, it is not the number of people that are affected by bullying or excessive aggression that should be the criterion for its consideration. The quantity of a problem is not the measure of its importance, even though busy personnel directors have innumerable demands on their time.

The way the problem is dealt with will eventually be known by a great number of people. All of them will use such examples to evaluate the organisation's ethos, and be influenced by the experience. Personnel officers and managers must satisfy themselves that reports of bullying are not symptoms of a wider problem inside the organisation. If they are, the situation is an opportunity for understanding, rather than a further drain on their time. If a doctor is making a diagnosis and ignores or misreads a symptom, the long-term consequences may be far more serious. Ignoring the symptoms in an organisation may also result in a demand to know why such a problem was not picked up much sooner.

Yet many establishments tolerate unacceptable behaviour because of the success and achievement of certain individuals. Some companies clearly base their success on the ruthlessness of their business practices. It is not surprising, therefore, that behaviour which makes one person successful can be damaging in terms of human relationships.

Ideally, it should be company policy for all individuals to make the effort to understand human relations at work and the part they play. There is certainly a clear need to differentiate between the areas of possible responsibility.

- An organisation's moral duty to understand human relations.
- Leaders at all levels committed to policies concerning the interpersonal relationships of all employees.
- Where such concern is reflected in creating the right ethos, good human relations become the expected responsibility of all employees.

157

- Prevention officers responsible for spotting the signs and helping to improve relationships when difficulties arise.
- Other individuals whose role, whether formalised or not, is to assess the situation once everything is already out of hand.

As part of the responsibility of understanding, all organisations, as a matter of course, would have to ask certain questions of their staff in order to learn from experience:

- What could we do to improve your working life?
- What have you learnt from your job that we need to keep in mind?
- What would aid a better understanding of the way in which we work together?
- When something goes wrong, how can we learn from the experience?
- How is aggression managed here?
- What is your way of managing stress?

This approach is saying: 'We value your experience and want to learn from it. We are not interested just in what you do, but in what you think.' If there are problems, it is everybody's responsibility to think together about what is going on. By asking its employees about their experience, an organisation engenders responsibility. It assumes intelligence, not stupidity. It does not just implement solutions which can foster a thoughtless, childlike work environment, but generates active involvement by the workforce by drawing on their adult capabilities.

Evaluating aggression

When one is trying to assess the extent of a problem, one valuable clue is the language used by the victim to describe the experience. The skills one needs to develop are skills that help one to differentiate types of aggression from the victims' reports. One person who moans: 'He's always getting at me' is not communicating the fear of someone who feels so threatened that you can find yourself becoming chilled as you listen to their detailed description of what the bully does. There again, people who are prone to exaggerate can dramatise the situation, whereas if you hear a bullying incident related in a straightforward way, it may reflect a far more serious problem.

When people speak of something that distresses them, and cry, it can demonstrate how deeply upset they are. This is different from individuals who tell you harrowing stories, but so coolly that you wonder what really is going on. In response to the first experience you may feel really moved; in the second you may feel puzzled, and even a little suspicious.

Rosemary, a bank clerk:

'I banged the desk once and shouted at him. He calmed down a bit and became more reasonable, but when I came out of the room, I knew I would suffer later. He had a phenomenal memory for things that were destructive. He wouldn't delegate. He didn't trust people. Paranoia, I suppose. He was out to get us because he thought we were out to get him.'

The idea of someone being 'out to get you' has images of extreme violence. But if you listen frequently enough to descriptions of the aggression fermenting beneath the polished veneer of many organisations, it will become clear that some very disturbed behaviour is enacted which would not be tolerated elsewhere. However, an individual's need for a job, and their concern with career prospects, may make them tolerate – albeit unwillingly – completely unacceptable conduct.

Many examples of bullying are from the top down. The aggression is manifested in arrogance which provokes potential conflict.

159

Sonia, a union official, found this pattern in her experience:

> 'The more senior a person is, the more difficult it is to get that individual to recognise that they are bullying subordinates. Their attitude is: "I am what I am . . . there's my record . . . I've always come through . . . if I've had a few casualties on the way, so what?"'

This defensive argument is very difficult to work with. Basically, the message is: My method works . . . this is how I am . . . take it or leave it. Stonewalling complaints in this fashion creates confrontation. It can also lead to disputes and the need for arbitration.

To help minimise the risk of one-sided attitudes, some companies have introduced evaluation methods which assess from the bottom up as well as from the top down. On a six-monthly or yearly basis, a leader's management skills are evaluated by his or her team, and vice versa. In theory this can establish a balance which gives subordinates the opportunity to feed back their experience of a superior, and any problems which may have arisen within the relationship.

Lies and truth

The truth, or course, can always be distorted. Where individuals disagree as to what is happening in a particular situation, it may be that they genuinely had different experiences. It may also be that the aggressor is lying, even though they may not be experiencing themselves as distorting the truth. If four people with no axe to grind describe a meeting, each will select different elements, and emphasise particular points. The same event will be reported differently even though the experience was without animosity. However, where representations and

160

reporting of behaviour are being dealt with, the possibility of distortion is ever present.

As we have already seen, many an incident that contains a bullying element takes place in private. Frequently, it becomes a matter of who is believed when a complaint is made. Consider Tom's experience as a systems analyst:

> 'Anything that had to be discussed meant that you had to be alone in his room where there were no witnesses. He would later insist to others publicly that you had said something which you had not, or he would publicly deny what he himself had said. On two occasions I went to see him, with a colleague, and reminded him of what he had said. The answer was, "Oh, I think you must have been mistaken. I certainly have no recollection of saying anything of the kind. You see, I couldn't have said that because . . ." The result was that I was the one made out to be the liar.'

It is a characteristic of some bullies to be tricky, evasive and uncompromising because they are trying to protect themselves at all costs. Equally important is their ability to attribute to an accuser the characteristics they themselves display, and to make any criticism seem unfounded; it is as if the person complaining has fabricated the situation. This slippery quality has implications for the way bullying in organisations is handled.

Where two or more people disagree about what is going on, it may not be possible to evaluate the truth on the basis of what is said. What may be more telling is what an arbiter in the situation *feels*. For example, if you are in that role, and while you are listening you feel unmoved by a person's distress, it may be that you are picking up something phoney in their story. What you must be alert to, in yourself as an arbiter, is that you do not react to other people's distress by switching off and feeling nothing at all. The evidence of your own experience of the individuals involved may give a more accurate picture than attempting to assess who is telling the truth.

Dealing with aggression

Many organisations develop policies and procedures for responding to difficulties arising from aggression. In dealing with bullying, however, any such policy must be born out of an understanding of the phenomenon itself. You can take statements about a bully; you can listen to both sides; but without an understanding of the way individuals and groups work, it will be hard to know how to proceed.

The phenomenon of bullying requires an understanding of the primitive elements in human nature: murderous feelings, aggression as a form of defence, and the potency and irrationality that accompany these elements. It also requires some understanding of group behaviour; how gangs work; what part rumour plays in organisations; the difficulties of establishing the truth in any given situation; and the way in which people attempt to establish alliances.

The culture of the organisation may have enabled the bully to flourish, for example. In areas involving education, where small departments are run with relative autonomy, the presence of a tyrannical or autocratic head may make the lives of the team below utterly miserable. That misery is perpetuated by the wider organisation.

An overall principal may have fifteen or twenty departments to manage and depend on individual heads to run them. All that may concern these people is that everything is going well, so anyone with a grievance risks an intolerable life if they go direct to the principal with their complaint. If the principal backs a more junior member of staff, they will risk not only undermining the authority of the head of department, but also a complete breakdown in relations. With a hundred other headaches to deal with, only in a major crisis would senior management intervene. In the meantime, a person in charge can continue to rule their fiefdom, and bully their staff, with apparent impunity.

Two lessons spring from this scenario. Anyone who has to arbitrate needs the capacity to tease out a problem. This means developing the skill to understand not only those to whom they feel sympathetic, but also those whose viewpoints and attitudes may differ, or even be anathema to them. Equally important is the ability to pick up clues which stem from an understanding of the psychology of conflict.

To take one example: if a person accused of bullying denies all knowledge of what is going on, it does not help to say, 'It's your word against his (or hers)'. More valuable is the ability to probe the situation with an open mind and wonder, 'What might lie behind this conflict?' or 'What is the history of your relationship?' Such questions do not accuse, they explore.

Linked to this exploratory mode is the demeanour adopted in situations which are highly charged. If it is possible – although it may not be – it is important to try to retain the capacity to stand back; to listen, reflect and think. Where extremes of fury, aggression and hatred are being dealt with, understanding what might be going on is a useful way of lowering the temperature. Where passion and anger are boiling up, it will be important to help those involved to think things through. This is a goal to be aimed for, although if the situation has gone beyond understanding, firmness and action will be required. A situation may be rendered safe only by calling a halt to it.

In some places of work, groups of people band together to work out a strategy to deal with a bully. This is how the staff of one school responded to problems with their headmaster:

'We desisted from further argument, kept absolutely silent, and adopted a policy of non-reaction. The

163

head's apparently self-satisfied smirk was replaced with a puzzled "what are they up to now?" expression, and although this strategy did nothing to alter the practical problems, we felt better because it was no longer the headmaster calling the tune.'

This course of action is interesting because it exemplifies the value of modifying a response, rather than attempting to change an individual's behaviour. Rather than reacting to provocation, which may be the response a bully hopes for, the group literally removed the satisfaction of confrontation. Obviously it is a powerful move to work in unison, although it straddles the fine line between collective action and bullying by a group. What distinguishes this action is that the response has been thought out, has realistic goals, and is a genuine attempt to bring group pressure to bear.

Just as many areas of responsibility may be outlined in a job description, so too can the problems of bullying and aggression be on the agenda of an organisation. It is reasonable to expect that good human relations should be an essential part of a manager's brief, and that they would expect to be told of instances of bullying in their department. This is not to say, of course, that they should seek out any behaviour that might be termed as bullying. Witch-hunts only create the fear that they would be intending to alleviate.

On the other hand, policies designed to protect employees can be used to threaten and intimidate. Such policies must strike a balance between protecting the rights of the individual, while retaining the capacity of managers and directors to exercise a healthy and just authority over others. Where a policy has the potential to undermine authority, it will create more harm in the organisation than the behaviour it was intended to control.

Any individual with a grudge may use a policy or procedure to threaten others and get them into trouble. Those in authority require training to distinguish between genuine complaints and more dubious attempts to malign or cast aspersions on a colleague – for example, to be able to spot an attempt to curry favour for oneself by throwing doubts on the integrity of another.

Agenda-free meetings

If there are problems which require understanding, consideration must be given to what type of platform might enable hidden agendas and complex relationships to be openly explored.

In a business meeting, the agreed agenda is often essential for dealing with matters allied to the performance of the organisation. It can, of course, be used to stifle discussion, or at least control its direction. If an organisation can tolerate examining what is really going on inside the working group, it will be necessary to move towards agenda-free meetings on a regular basis so that any problems can be brought to the surface and examined. Difficulties that have been disregarded or kept under wraps may surface on the back of other issues.

It is because of the fear of what might come up that some organisations maintain tight agendas. Consequently, dissent is expressed in private. Problems such as low morale and difficulties or disagreements within departments are not examined, so while everything may appear fine on the surface, an organisation may not be flourishing, but just getting by. As with an individual, failure to examine its own workings may result in a failure to operate at full potential, and internal conflicts may absorb the psychological resources of the workforce. Looking to the future, an agenda-free meeting may make the difference between a smooth-running organisation and one which just hobbles along. It is also a way in which the impact of aggression on an organisation can be examined and worked through.

A healthy organisation

Where the workforce thinks together about problems as they arise, the environment will not lend itself to bullying. In such democratic organisations, the prevailing consideration is co-operation and concern. They recognise that it is a basic need for someone at work to feel that their contribution is valued and important; that teams work best where individuals have a role, and where there is respect for their ideas and experience. Most importantly, problems can be looked at and worked on without an employee fearing humiliation, or being frowned on. Obvious though it may seem, all individuals are different, with different qualities. Organisations that can tolerate these differences are more likely to run smoothly, because it is not their expectation that everyone will be the same.

The notion of a healthy organisation is akin to the notion of a healthy family. There will be values that promote good human relations, not conflict; an ethos built on individuals taking responsibility which means that control becomes less important. In this climate, problems can be looked at and understood. However, it is the struggle towards these kinds of ideals that is more important than achieving them. It is this that reflects not only an establishment that is thinking about itself and its workforce, but one that is thinking about creating the kind of environment in which it is rewarding to work. These organisations usually promote success, commitment and good human relations. In such an environment, a bully has no place.

Neil Crawford
1992

12
Managing People Properly

Change is the law of life. And those
who look only to the past or the present
are certain to miss the future.
J. F. Kennedy

For any organisation, the most positive way forward, through the 1990s and beyond, is clearly linked to a deeper understanding of itself and all those it employs. Every individual gets a kick out of being praised, so creating an ethos in which people can feel valued, respected and encouraged is one of the ways in which every organisation can fulfil its role. It is also plain, however, that wherever such values are not already in existence (and if they were universally applied, this book would not need to have been written), careful consideration must be given to ways of achieving these aims.

Research carried out by one of the largest teams in the world looking at occupational stress has established that bullying is potentially the most potent source of stress which causes people to stay away from work through fear. Adding to his team's findings as Professor of Organisational Psychology at the University of Manchester Institute of Science and Technology (UMIST), Cary Cooper provides an important clue to good management:

'The nature of the boss–subordinate relationship is an extremely important one because it is almost like a substitute parent–child relationship. When we are children we look to our parents for reward; we try to do things to please them. Employees do the same thing

167

in the work environment: they try to get rewarded by the boss. But in Britain we really are abysmal at understanding how vital it is for an employee that there is a good relationship between bosses and their subordinates. To manage people properly, you have to value them, make them feel important and reward them for doing things right.'

In this respect, both the bullied and the bully desire recognition for the same reason. If the confidence was there in the first place, the need for recognition would be tempered to a level which was actually attainable. This final chapter will look at some of the steps that can be taken to create a happy, successful and competitive atmosphere in which everyone can work without feeling threatened. Contrary to popular belief, it is not technical or academic knowledge, or even sales or organisational skills, which form the hub of a successful workplace. These ingredients are extremely important in their place, but the real key to quality is the ability to know how to manage people properly.

Getting it wrong
Sue, a civil servant:

'He never praises good work, unless you are his "favourite". He tells everybody else that unless he says anything to the contrary, we can asssume that our work is satisfactory. As a result, we never feel valued as employees, only that we are managing to survive until the next time. He never comes round voluntarily to see how our work is progressing, or ask if anyone has any problems. He likes people to go and consult him in his office. In fact the more you ask for his advice, the better he likes it. It seems to reinforce his idea of himself as "management". If he wants to tell us something, he sends round a memo which we all have to sign, even though his office is in the same room as ours, and he works about six feet away from the nearest employee. It is not about helping people, it is about having power over them, and keeping them in a subordinate position where they can never challenge that power by becoming fitted for promotion.'

When Norah took up her post with a German company making electrical appliances in the UK as secretary to the personnel manager, she soon discovered the high turnover rate her position had:

'Soon after I arrived I learnt that my predecessor had left after only a few months under my new boss, and several secretaries before that had walked out. My boss had previously been a secretary to the personnel manager herself, and worked her way up to the job she now held within the organisation. Her real skill was in organising a department and recruiting, but she wasn't a people person. In fact she could barely be civil.

'Quite often I'd be stopped in the corridor by other members of staff, and because I'm interested in people, I'd listen, then tell them to drop into the office to pick up a sickness certificate, or whatever it was that they wanted. If my boss saw me talking to anyone, she'd walk up and down and let out an exasperated sigh, before telling me that I wasn't paid to talk to other employees. She said it could be thought that as someone from personnel, I was discussing other people's personal matters. I remember being amazed at her reaction because I thought a department like ours should have an air of approachability. As it was, staff didn't like coming into the office when she was there.

'Gradually, she started to take it out on me. Every morning she used to growl a sort of greeting. The rest of the time she constantly hovered over me, or inspected my "out" tray. If I was doing the filing, she would walk past and ask me to type a letter. If I was typing a letter, she would insist that I caught up on the filing. I never knew where I was. I felt like a junior typist who was only there to make the coffee and be told what to do. Just over a year later, my stomach churned every time I was in her presence, and I felt very knocked down by the way she treated me, so I decided to get another job and leave. It took six years for me to recover my self-confidence, and that was entirely due to my present boss. He doesn't *tell* me to do things all the time, he *asks* if I can do them instead. His tone of voice is so different, too. With him there's always a cheery "Good morning". It gets the day off to a good start.'

Was Norah's previous boss promoted beyond her capabilities, or promoted because of who she knew rather than what she knew? Either way, it seems self-defeating to risk even one area of an organisation by failing to carry out an early and accurate assessment of the individual. Promoting this type of person into any sort of supervisory role, with the added responsibility for the psychological well-being of other employees, is likely to prove counterproductive. Being given a job and told to get on with it, without skilful training in the subtleties of how to be an effective boss, is imposing an unfair expectation on any individual who may never have benefited from the parental example of social skills. In addition, if the bully feels overstretched by the demands being made, and unable to cope with their new role, the other employees bear the brunt.

It seems ironic that when a company is thinking of investing a lot of money in a piece of new machinery, it carries out research into what is available to make sure that the final choice has the right specifications. For an organisation to run smoothly and effectively, research into the people who are going to operate within it is equally important. If things go wrong through a lack of thorough research, it is the weak link in a human chain that will require the most costly and time-consuming repair. The emphasis on people skills should clearly equal the emphasis placed on technical ability if those destructive character traits are to be picked up before they begin to undermine others.

But the criterion at a promotion interview may be, for example, that the applicant has to be well qualified and experienced: a good operator in their own right who gets results. Will this proven self-performer be any good at managing people just because their skill in the sales area has been second to none? In a recruitment interview, a representative picture of a bully is unlikely to emerge without a line of questioning designed to penetrate the image of best behaviour that all of us can create for an important occasion.

The fact that a bullying style is something which can be covert, and therefore difficult to identify, means that it is not going to be revealed through references or an interview unless you know what you are looking for. Good listening skills, a pleasant attitude and an even temperament are some of the qualities required to help create an atmosphere in which people wish to remain. Recognition of any idiosyncrasy at an early stage will help to evaluate the needs of the potential bully in relation to those of other employees. Failure to do so presents a serious risk.

Consequences of getting it wrong

- Industrial unrest
- Lack of motivation
- Declining productivity
- Declining profit
- People feel redundant. It stifles their creativity. ('If that's the way he feels, I'm not going to *bother* to offer any ideas'.)

- Staff are demoralised ('If I can't do anything right, what is the point in making an effort?')
- A decline in the standard of staff relations. ('We're always being given a hard time, but nobody seems to notice.')
- No organisational structure because it is all down to one individual. ('Who are we supposed to turn to when the boss is a bully?')

Protecting the bullied

Faced with the bully who has infiltrated an organisation, it is important to remember that those who have been subjected to this person's aggressive behaviour will need reassurance. They will want to feel protected from the figure who has – sometimes for years – haunted their daily lives. They will need to know:

- That the bully is being transferred to another section or another department on the same site, or to another branch of the organisation.
- That whatever happens, they will remain safe.
- That until further notice, any attempt by the bully to make direct contact with previous colleagues, other than through an appointed third person, will result in disciplinary measures.
- That this person is made fully aware of the effect their behaviour has been having on others.
- That the bully is being helped to unlearn his or her aggressive behaviour style – and how.
- That until those responsible for human relations are satisfied that the individual concerned has been successfully retrained, he or she will not be put in a position of managing other employees.

In a small company or organisation, this line of approach may prove impossible because there is nowhere to move the bullying employee to. Nevertheless, it will be equally important to recognise the needs of all those involved. If there is no workable solution, and the bully has to be asked to step down, it will be vital to offer counselling support to help restore confidence among the employees who remain.

Where all parties remain, a firm line must be taken against the bully to let them know that this is the way they are perceived by others, and this is the impact their behaviour is having. It may be that the bully's response, together with a consistently poor record of relationships at work, indicates that any attempt at retraining would be unlikely to achieve change.

If there is no acceptance of the part they have played, for example, then dismissal may be the only answer. It is self-acknowledgement that is the critical turning point – indeed, the first step in the healing process. Effective counselling, either from within or outside the organisation, is important to help the aggressor realise what it is that has happened to them in the past that has made them a bully (see Chapter 6).

Another positive move in the direction of protecting individual employees is the introduction of the upward appraisal. After all, who knows the quality of a manager better than those being managed? Despite the fact that this type of attitude survey is still largely untried in Britain (but not uncommon in the USA), it presents the opportunity for an untapped source of information in many organisations.

The prevailing attitude in many hierarchical British companies is that only bosses are entitled to assess the performance of staff through appraisals or annual reports. Introducing assessment from the bottom up has, until recently, been an unpopular proposition, largely because of the fear that asking staff what they think of their managers is also asking them what they think of the company for which they work. However, organisations which have recently taken their courage in both hands

173

and introduced upward assessments have found that managers now consider much more carefully the way in which they relate to their staff.

Surveys of this nature, conducted anonymously, present a golden opportunity to the disaffected to air their griev-ances. In the case of one well-known British retailing company, for example, upward assessments identified some basic needs: for training in interpersonal skills; for the ability to discuss personal difficulties, to talk openly and honestly at an early stage when performance problems arise; to make the most of individuals who might otherwise be written off – but who might, instead, be 'turned round'.

Changing behaviour patterns

Once a bully has been identified by the organisation – either through the selection process or through complaints from individuals – the opportunity is there to offer this person help and support. It ought, perhaps, to be an obligation. After all, the bully was appointed in the first place, and surely every organisation which takes on that responsibility is answerable for the psychological safety of *all* its employees?

In his enlightening book Marcus Sieff – *On Management: the Marks & Spencer Way*, published in 1990, Lord Sieff of Brimpton draws a contrast between attitudes to human relations in Marks & Spencer in his father's time, and attitudes today. The manager at the Hammersmith store where Lord Sieff trained was critical, never gave praise, rarely, if ever, used the words 'Thank you', and had no rapport with his staff. When the young trainee attacked his attitude, his father merely described him as 'one of the old school'. The following passage from Lord Sieff's book describes a similar problem but a very different approach:

If he is taken in hand in time, a manager who is bad with his staff can be taught and reformed. When I was

174

personnel director, I came across a manager who, though in many ways adept at his job, irritated his staff. His main trouble was that he considered his own ego at the expense of theirs and was censorious. When I asked his supervisors for their account of the previous week's sales, and they were telling me that they had sold about eight dozen of this or that item, he would interrupt and say, 'No, we did not – it was eight dozen and four.' This sort of interruption happened constantly as we went round the sales floors.

I looked into the situation at the store and found there was a high turnover of staff; some of them obviously could not stand him. I decided to remove him from the medium-size store he managed and make him deputy to one of our best managers who was running one of our bigger stores. He did not take too kindly to the move since it was a demotion, but he did as he was advised. He learnt a great deal and became the manager for many years of one of our largest and fastest developing stores, where he did an excellent job. Perhaps he would have had similar success with the Hammersmith manager if we had known as much then as we do now about how to help people help themselves.

Good human relations at work do not mean being soft in one's treatment of people, but being fair and frank with them, giving praise where praise is due and constructive criticism when such is justified. This is important.

But this is a skill which rarely comes naturally to a bullying boss. The Marks & Spencer anecdote is an example of how essential management techniques can be learnt through another person's successful approach. Offering an alternative role model to the one which has influenced the bully in earlier life can be an effective method of retraining. It is learning by experience, and by receiving confirmation in the process that this new way of managing people is not only getting a positive and friendly response, it is also producing good results.

Old habits die hard, of course, particularly habits that have been instilled from an early age. Successfully retraining the bully means going back to basics. If you like, it means offering them the good parental example they themselves probably never experienced, by teaching the simple social skills that make it easier to get on and do the job without destroying the self-esteem of other employees. Another quality which the bully will probably need to learn is the art of empathy. In any work environment, the ability to understand – or imagine – what others might need is invaluable.

Part of the organisation's role in helping to reform any employee with a bullying, aggressive style is to take on board the psychological profile of a person who behaves in this way towards other employees. Asserting themselves through overpowering others may be the only way they have learnt to defend their position from anyone they perceive as some sort of threat. Once they have acknowledged the effect their behaviour is having, part of the recovery process will be to reassure them that they can still have a future within the organisation.

This may be possible without creating a new post, simply by moving the person into another sphere which can benefit from their previous skills while the unlearning process is put into place. It will give everyone an important breathing space. Offering techniques in stress management and non-aggressive assertiveness are other essential strands in changing the behaviour pattern of an established bully. These techniques will, of course, be equally valuable to those who have been bullied.

Counselling, courses in personal development, training in the importance of social skills, are also part of the repair package which must be made available by any organisation in which bullying is identified – indeed, by every organisation which cares about the people it employs. The peer-group approach is a further option for helping the bully understand the need for change within the community. Bullies who have benefited from the group therapy they have sought out for themselves would undoubtedly feel less isolated if they were not metaphorically put behind iron bars but helped, with others like them, through peer-group counselling, or by some other emotional support team operating within the workplace.

Until such procedures are put into place, it is to be hoped that wider recognition of bullying, and what it actually involves when it takes place among adults at work, may encourage some perpetrators to seek help for themselves. It is important to make it publicly known that help is as available for the bully as it is for those who have been singled out for the bully's aggression. It has to be asked, of course, whether that person will really wish to be identified with a label that has such a stigma.

It must be made clear that recognising bullying for what it really is does not represent a Them and Us situation, but a socialising process backed up by a network of support offering help, understanding and advice. As in the case of anyone affected by this experience, the bully also needs to be assured that disclosure will be treated in confidence.

To those in charge of corporate spending, of course, the prospect of such costly investment in people alone might seem very idealistic. Looking after the psychological well-being of a workforce will mean considerable saving in the long term. The people concerned will be better equipped to concentrate on producing the quality results which ensure high financial returns.

Professor Cary Cooper, UMIST:

'One of the most significant predictors and sources of stress in the workplace is the boss and the way he manages people. The really rather sad thing we have found is that quite a few bosses manage by punishment and not by reward. They don't tell people when they do a good job, but they certainly do let them know when they do a bad job. And that, for a lot of people, is consistent punishment.'

People who go to work are not pieces of machinery requiring an occasional oiling to keep them running effectively. Human beings need a drip-feed of praise and encouragement to know that the contribution they make is valued as the most critical part of the production process.

Andrew, an accountant:

'As a person who has been bullied, it is important to me to have someone else say "That was good". Not "That was quite good", or "That was good but it could have been even better if . . .", or "You've got a lot of work to do before you can sit back". Without recognition for what one is, through the acknowledgement of achievement, or of the contribution that has been made, you are not fed the energy needed to continue with enthusiasm. It seems to me now that I've grown to expect to be put down, and it makes further efforts ever harder.'

Trust, courtesy and positive feedback, even on a standard performance, will not only help an individual to feel valued, it will help them to feel more comfortable with the way they are. Knowing that their work is important, and that they are doing a good job, may encourage them to achieve greater things.

Getting it right

Norah, the secretary to the personnel manager who left her job because she felt she was being bullied, now works for a Director of Human Resources in a leading employment agency. Her self-confidence has been rebuilt by a new boss who is well versed in social skills:

178

'By the time I left my previous job, she had picked on me so often that I was full of self-doubt. It would take me at least an hour to produce a simple, two-line letter of reply.

My new boss will say to me, "I'll leave you to sort out the layout of this letter, you do it so well." Then I feel I can, of course. I remember one day he put a lot of files on my desk and said, "I don't know how we're going to work this out, but I couldn't place the job anywhere else. The buck stops here and *we* have taken on this new responsibility." I immediately felt part of it and involved, and I knew that if I didn't understand, I could consult him. In the end I had to take on the whole thing and I quite enjoyed that. It made me feel really valued because he was happy to leave that responsibility with me, to trust me to do it properly and get it right.

'He asks my opinions, too, and that makes me feel just as important to the running of the department as he is. It also gives me a feeling of confidence, and being more involved not only gives me greater job satisfaction, it means I'm more enthusiastic. He also asks if I think I can do things, and rarely gives me any typing just before going-home time. His tone is cheerful, too, which makes all the difference to the working day. When I've done a job he'll say, "Thank you very much, that's really good", or "I like the way you've typed that report." When he asks for something, he never forgets to say "please". On one occasion, he introduced me to a senior colleague who came to the office and he said, "You don't know Norah, do you?" She obviously didn't know I was his secretary, so when she shook my hand she said, "What are you? Do you work with Stuart or for him?" At that point my boss replied, "Well actually, she does both." It made me feel really special.'

It is commitment, not overbearing authority, that achieves the aims of every organisation, but whether attempting to undo the original damage, or maintaining standards which already exist, it is essential to follow up praise and encouragement with action that in some way provides psychological reward. Through his research into stress at work, Professor Cooper has become convinced that 'the key ingredient missing in working life is how to manage people properly'. He has also found that very few companies in the UK provide training programmes which teach the basic social skills required in a working environment to help bosses manage their employees effectively.

In the case of the bully, and sometimes the bullied, the following examples represent experiences of behaviour that may never have been encountered at the learning stage in early life. Basic though they may appear – almost childish, even to the adult eye – these simple skills, when used appropriately in the workplace, will not only help people to feel good about themselves, they will mobilise contribution to the aims and goals of the organisation.

- The cheerful smile which 'gets the day off to a good start'.
- Remembering to say 'please' and 'thank you'.
- Listening to what other people have to say.
- Offering genuine praise and encouragement when you like what they do.
- Knowing how to reward them so that they want to go on producing good results.
- Helping others to feel wanted by making it known that they are equally involved.
- Making it clear what you expect from their work, but if a problem arises, explaining how things have gone wrong.

Being able to imagine what you would want in someone else's shoes, faced with the same set of circumstances, will help win the commitment and support of other people. Just like those on the other side of the counter, people at work not only need to enjoy the experience, they also need to know that they have the right to raise any concern and expect a considered response. After all, the customer who is ill-treated and ignored usually crosses the high street to shop elsewhere. If it happens too often, it is the sales that also suffer.

> 'You don't manage people by demeaning them, devaluing them and putting them down. That's the most ineffective way of managing human beings. If you don't manage your employees well, they'll leave, so you'd better be good people-managers, otherwise you're going to be out of business.' – Professor Cary Cooper, 'Whose Fault Is It Anyway?', BBC Radio 4, 1991

HELPING YOURSELF
Changing the climate

- Put the needs of people before profit.
- Make codes of practice quite clear – i.e. what is acceptable behaviour within the organisation, and what isn't.
- Offer counselling support for all staff.

Providing protection

If a member of staff is unhappy, offer a procedure which allows them to take their grievance to someone other than the person above – to someone else within the organisation who has the power to take appropriate action. If the individual is not content to take their complaint to their immediate personnel officer, make it known in staff manuals, or on noticeboards, that a complaint about bullying, or anything else of a serious nature, may be confidentially directed towards the personnel manager or divisional manager. This will help to reduce the threat of recrimination.

The obvious response will be to put the matter into a grievance pro-cedure, but it is important to take into account the feelings of those who complain about being bullied. Recognise the real difficulty they will have in confronting the bully face to face at a formal meeting.

In cases of regular sick leave, make it known to employees that GPs can be specific about the reasons for any stress-related illness, and that the matter will be treated in complete confidence.

In schools, introduce a team structure which offers a support mechanism for all staff. In this way, a teacher who feels bullied by a head, or head of department, will have a number of channels through which he or she can make an official complaint. From the top down these should include deputy heads, heads of faculty, year heads, year group tutors. The team approach also means that all managers can become responsible for checking the behaviour of a potential bully or, if necessary, raising specific complaints with the local Education Authority.

Where might bullying exist?

Many clues have been offered in this book for identifying the warning signs which can reveal a problem of bullying at work. Listening to employees becomes even more important in these circumstances, as does the need to see through the euphemisms which are often used to disguise this type of conduct.

Checking for clues

- Watch the workplace for a change in atmosphere among staff. When cheerfulness turns to virtual silence, this is a bad sign. Bear in mind that a 'walking the floor' style of management will be counterproductive if the boss is a bully.

- Use stress/culture audits or upward assessments to identify problem areas.
- Introduce agenda-free meetings to provide a platform for troubled staff.
- In exit interviews, include the specific question: 'Have you experienced bullying in this organisation?'

Asking the individuals

- Inquire about physical symptoms and state of health.
- Check on morale.
- If this person says they are being constantly criticised, do the allegations tally with reports on their performance in previous appraisals, reports or references?
- Have they, or has somebody else within their area, recently joined this working group?
- Could the bully have been put under too much pressure to achieve results?

Helping people to recover

- Take their complaint seriously.
- Offer Employee Assistance Programmes or other counselling. Both will provide invaluable support for both the bullied and the bully, as well as for all the other personal problems people bring to work.
- Personnel officers effectively trained in in-depth counselling can provide important back-up support, as can selected members of management and union representatives within an organisation.
- Non-aggressive assertiveness courses and training in

stress management will help both bullied and bully to cope more effectively in the future.

- Offer retraining through courses which specifically develop the social and interpersonal skills mentioned in Chapter 12.
- Encourage the establishment of work councils.
- Remember that ACAS can assist employers and employees to develop stable and effective relationships at work which seek to eradicate all forms of harassment. Advice is also offered to individuals, employers and trade unions on any aspect of industrial relations (including bullying) and on employment policies.

Endpiece

Every institution not only carries within it the seeds of its own dissolution but prepares the way for its most hated rival.

W. R. Inge, Dean of St Paul's Cathedral, 1911–34

If the culture of an organisation is aimed at getting the best out of people, it is quite clear that this is not being achieved in many British and American organisations. If anything, the apparent scepticism about – and the reluctance of management adequately to confront – the widespread phenomenon of bullying at work is continuing to alienate large numbers of people from their organisations. Yet what sort of workplace can really wish to condone a form of behaviour which engenders fear in its employees?

There are always those who will put forward the argument that making snide remarks, or jokes at other people's expense, is merely 'part of human nature'. Office banter which is not really designed to offend is undoubtedly different to the persistent downgrading of human beings by an individual in a position of power. This is where 'normal' behaviour crosses the boundary into bullying.

Where the problem of bullying exists, and someone is willing to tackle it, the bully will have to be addressed and prevailed upon to change. In some ways, it is a shared responsibility to try and get it right. Exploring the more subtle aspects of human nature is certainly an option open to every individual. However, while employees are answerable to employers, the ultimate responsibility for engineering change in the workplace lies with each and every organisation.

It takes much more than the latest technology, good financial reward or an aesthetically pleasing environment to create the right atmosphere in which people can not only enjoy making an important and valued contribution, but also feel safe when they go to work. The psychology of interpersonal relationships affects us all, but especially in the workplace, where people have to live together on a daily basis for no better reason than to earn a living. Their level of commitment will depend on the attitude of those in authority. For an organisation to be effective, it must understand the importance of matching its own expectations with those of the individual.

Inaction in the face of a bully can be likened to the response of the parent who always believes he or she knows best when another child in the family complains of unfair treatment. Yet this inaction is not seen by large numbers of employees merely as sheer incompetence, but as an organised conspiracy to keep any unpleasantness posed by the situation well and truly under wraps. This response to what is perceived as injustice confirms a clear requirement for organisations to align themselves with the role expected of a positive parent.

At present there is an absence of formal training in the basic skills of good parenting, and though training in management style is high on the agenda of many organisations, as yet it does not appear to have struck the right balance. While organisations are unconsciously regarded by many employees as substitute parents, the culture must surely reflect an attempt to provide a good role model to help nurture a confident and healthy workforce.

The effect of earlier family experiences on a person's adult life are often dismissed as a cliché, yet it is quite clear that these relationships can be the underlying cause of stress at work, and of potential conflict with authority figures. In a working environment, it may be a matter of chance and combination of personalities which determines who is the bullied or who is the bully. The desire for recognition is the motivation of both parties. The responsibility of the organisation is to comprehend this desire; to equate the healthy use of authority with that of a fair parent figure who not only balances criticism with praise, but also makes those for whom it is responsible feel cared for, as well as valued for who they are and what they have to offer. Understanding what it is that people might want is a realistic aim for any organisation which regards quality as its ultimate goal.

Charlotte, a civil servant:

'It is incredible that management has not yet got the message that the misery continues, even after detailed reports and complaints to Personnel. In our place of work one person has been transferred; another has been sacked; one other continues to be attacked by the bully via the annual reporting system just as I was; another has been moved from one part of the office to another section because she was said to be "upsetting people and turning them against the woman in charge". It feels like a conspiracy to keep us all under control, but how long are they prepared to allow this to go on?'

Further Reading

Chapter 6

Sigmund Freud, *The Future of an Illusion*, in James Strachey (ed.), *The Standard Edition of the Complete Psychological Works of Sigmund Freud* (London: Hogarth Press, 1961, vol. 21).

Erich Fromm, *The Anatomy of Human Destructiveness* (London: Jonathan Cape, 1974), p. 236.

Leonard Shengold, *Soul Murder* (New Haven, CT and London: Yale University Press, 1989).

Gregory Bateson, *Steps to an Ecology of Mind* (London: Paladin, 1987).

R. D. Laing, *The Divided Self* (London: Tavistock, 1960).

Harvey Cleckley, *The Mask of Sanity* (Saint Louis, MI: C. V. Mosby, 1964).

Willy Gross-Mayer, Eliot Slater and Martin Roth, *Clinical Psychiatry* (Baltimore, MD: Williams & Wilkins, 1969).

Richard Hunter and Ida Macalpine, *Three Hundred Years of Psychiatry (1535–1860)* (London: Oxford University Press).

D. Lykkens, 'A Study of Anxiety in the Sociopath's Personality', in T. R. Sarbin (ed.), *Studies in Behaviour Pathology* (New York: Holt, Rinehart & Winston, 1962).

Cathy Widom, 'Interpersonal and Personal Construct Systems in Psychopaths', *Journal of Consulting and Clinical Psychology*, 44, 1976, pp. 614–23.

Anthony Storr, *Human Destructiveness* (London: Sussex University Press, 1972), pp. 34–7.

Neil Crawford, *On Groups* (London: Tavistock Clinic Paper No. 63, 1987, unpublished).

D. W. Winnicott, *Home Is Where We Start From* (Harmondsworth: Pelican, 1986), p. 81.

Chapter 8

Neil Crawford, *Envy and Rivalry at Work* (London: Tavistock Clinic Paper No. 24, 1985, unpublished).

Karen Horney, *Self Analysis* (New York and London: W. W. Norton, 1968).

Chapter 11

Neil Crawford, *Democracy in Organisations* (London: Tavistock Clinic Paper No. 36, 1987, unpublished).

Neil Crawford, *Power and Powerlessness in Organisations* (London: Tavistock Clinic Paper No. 52, 1987, unpublished).

Chapter 12

Marcus Sieff, *On Management: The Marks & Spencer Way* (London: Weidenfeld & Nicolson, 1990), p. 67.

Routes to Recovery

Counselling

At some time in their lives, most people may find it difficult to cope and need help. Counselling provides an opportunity to explore difficulties and problems in a safe environment. Sharing thoughts and feelings leads to self-understanding. This provides the potential for dealing with problems and new challenges. Counselling is carried out in confidence.

Westminster Pastoral Foundation:
Contact its London headquarters to find out the name of your nearest WPF counselling service or affiliated centre:

23, Kensington Square, London W8 5HN; Tel.: 071 937 6956

Relate
(formerly known as Marriage Guidance) can help with relationship problems. Local branches can be found in your local telephone directory.

Scottish Institute of Human Relationships, 56 Albany Street, Edinburgh EH1 3QU; Tel. 031 556 6454

Therapy

In practice, counselling and psychotherapy overlap, although psychotherapy tends to explore more deep-seated personal issues by dealing with old hurts. It can help you to become aware of patterns that may have become unconscious and negative habits. Getting to know yourself better, and dealing with any pain that has been carried through from the past, is a healing process which helps to expand your capacity to enjoy life more in the present. Many health-care workers within the NHS train to high standards of practice within this field, and it is worth finding out about the psychotherapy provision in your area. For further information contact:

The Adlerian Society of Great Britain, 11 Osbourne House, 414 Wimbledon Park Road, London SW19; Tel. 081 789 8086

The British Association of Psychotherapists, 121 Hendon Lane, London N3 3PR; Tel. 081 346 1747

The London Centre for Psychotherapy, 19 Fitzjohn's Avenue, London NW3 5JY; Tel. 071 435 0873

Psychoanalysis

British Psycho-Analytical Society, 63 New Cavendish Street, London W1; Tel. 071 580 4952 – for Freudian and Kleinian analysts working throughout the country.

The Group Analytic Practice, 88 Montague Mansions, London W1H 1LF; Tel. 071 935 3103/3085

Society of Analytical Psychology, 1 Daleham Gardens, London NW3; Tel. 071 435 7696 – for Jungian analysts.

Within the NHS, psychoanalytic psychotherapy is the most frequently practised. It does not base itself on free association and is often time-limited. This less intense form of treatment is suitable for many emotional problems. For further details contact:

The Tavistock Clinic, 120 Belsize Lane, London NW3; Tel. 071 435 7111 – this is an NHS national centre for many forms of analysis and family therapy.

The Women's Therapy Centre, 6 Manor Gardens, London N7; Tel. 071 263 6200

Group Therapy

Contact The British Association of Psychotherapists or The Institute of Group Analysis

The Institute of Group Analysis
1 Daleham Gardens, London NW3
Tel: 071 431 2693

The British Association of Psychotherapists
37 Maplesbury Road, London NW2 4HJ
Tel: 081 452 9823

Organisations and Addresses

ACAS Advisory Service
27 Wilton Street, London SW1X 7AZ; Tel. 071 210 3000

ACAS (Scotland)
Franborough House, 123 Bothwell Street, Glasgow G2 7JR; Tel. 041 204 2677

ACAS (Wales)
Phase 1, Ty Glas Road, Llanishen, Cardiff CF4 5PH; Tel. 0222 762636

Regional offices of ACAS can be located through their London headquarters. See local telephone directories for Citizens' Advice Bureaux and Industrial Tribunal offices.

Equal Opportunities Commission
Overseas House, Quay Street, Manchester M3 3HN

National Council for Civil Liberties
21 Tabard Street, London SE1 4LA

The Suzy Lamplugh Trust (for assertiveness training courses)
14 East Sheen Avenue, London SW14 8AS

TUC
Congress House, Great Russell Street, London WC1

The Industrial Society
    (For all types of management training)
48 Bryanstone Square, London W1H 7LN

General Reading

Berne, Eric, *Games People Play* (Harmondsworth: Penguin,)

Cooper, Cary L., and others, *Living With Stress* (Harmondsworth: Penguin, 1988)

De Bono, Edward, *Conflicts: A Better Way to Resolve Them* (Harmondsworth: Pelican, 1986)

Harvey-Jones, Sir John, *Making It Happen* (London: Fontana 1989)

Klein, David and Aldous, Joan, *Social Stress and Family Development* (Hove: Guildford Press, 1988)

Knowles, Jane, *Know Your Own Mind* (London: Pandora, 1991)

Lamplugh, Diana, *Beating Aggression* (London: Weidenfeld & Nicolson, 1988)

Meth, Richard, *Men in Therapy: The Challenge of Change* (Hove: Guildford Press, 1990)

Miller, Alice, *The Drama of Being a Child* (London: Virago, 1987)

Miller, Alice, *For Your Own Good* (London: Virago, 1987)

Miller, Alice, *Banished Knowledge* (London: Virago, 1990)

Morita, Akio, *Made in Japan* (London: Fontana, 1988)

Reynolds, Bob, *The 100 Best Companies to Work for in the UK* (London: Fontana, 1989)

Rogers, Buck, *The I.B.M. Way* (London: Harper & Row, 1989)

Marcus Sieff, *On Management: The Marks & Spencer Way* (London: Weidenfeld & Nicolson, 1990)

Skynner, Robin, and Cleese, John, *Families and How to Survive Them* (London: Mandarin, 1990)

Storr, Anthony, *Human Aggression* (New York: Bantam Books, 1970)

Suttie, Ian, *The Origins of Love and Hate* (London: Free Association Books, 1988)

YOU JUST DON'T UNDERSTAND
Women and Men in Conversation

Deborah Tannen

At last, the book that explains why we find it difficult to talk to the opposite sex.

Why do so many women feel that men don't tell them anything, but just lecture and criticise? Why do so many men feel that women nag them and never get to the point? Why, even when they live under the same roof, do women and men seem to inhabit different worlds?

In this pioneering book Deborah Tannen shows us how women and men talk in profoundly different ways, for profoundly different reasons. While women use language primarily to make connections and reinforce intimacy, men use it to preserve their independence and negotiate status. The result? Genuine confusion.

You Just Don't Understand strikes resounding chords of recognition and shows us how, once we understand our differences, we can really begin to talk to each other.

'Deborah Tannen combines a novelist's ear for the way people speak with a rare power of original analysis . . . fascinating' – *Oliver Sacks*

BREAKING DOWN THE WALL OF SILENCE
To Join the Waiting Child

Alice Miller

In this pioneering new book, Alice Miller works towards demolishing the wall of silence which surrounds the sufferings of early childhood as they affect everyday life, politics, the media, psychiatry and psychotherapy.

An infant's trust and dependency on its parents, its longing to be loved and be able to love in return, are boundless. To exploit this dependency, to confuse a child's longings and abuse its trust by pretending that this is somehow 'good for' it, Alice Miller condemns as a criminal act, committed time and again out of ignorance and the refusal to change. 'Today I know that we cannot be free if we forget, relativise or excuse the brutality and horrors suffered in childhood. I want to release the memories blocked in me. I want to remember what I chose to forget and I want to know why I did so.'

The essential first stage in this healing process is *feeling* the truth of our experience. Only this, Alice Miller writes, can enable us 'to recognise childhood events and resolve their consequences so that we can lead a conscious, responsible life. If we know and feel what happened to us then, we will never wish to harm ourselves or others now'.

Virago also publish *The Untouched Key: Tracing Childhood Trauma in Creativity and Destructiveness*, *The Drama of Being a Child*, *Banished Knowledge: Facing Childhood Injuries* and *For Your Own Good: The Roots of Violence in Child Rearing*.

Now you can order superb titles directly from Virago

☐	The Memory Bird	Caroline Malone *et al.*	£7.99
☐	Breaking Down the Wall of Silence	Alice Miller	£7.99
☐	What's Really Going On Here	Susie Orbach	£7.99
☐	Strong at the Broken Places	Lynne Sanford	£8.99
☐	Talking from 9 to 5	Deborah Tannen	£8.99
☐	You Just Don't Understand	Deborah Tannen	£8.99

Please allow for postage and packing: **Free UK delivery.**
Europe; add 25% of retail price; Rest of World; 45% of retail price.

To order any of the above or any other Virago titles, please call our credit card orderline or fill in this coupon and send/fax it to:

Virago, 250 Western Avenue, London, W3 6XZ, UK.
Fax 020 8324 5678   Telephone 020 8324 5516

☐ I enclose a UK bank cheque made payable to Virago for £ ....

☐ Please charge £.............. to my Access, Visa, Delta, Switch Card No.

☐☐☐☐☐☐☐☐☐☐☐☐☐☐☐☐☐☐☐

Expiry Date ☐☐☐☐   Switch Issue No. ☐☐

NAME (Block letters please) ....

ADDRESS ....

....

....

Postcode ....Telephone ....

Signature ....

Please allow 28 days for delivery within the UK. Offer subject to price and availability.

Please do not send any further mailings from companies carefully selected by Virago ☐